THE

ARMC

ANARC

HIST'S

THE ARMCHAIR ANARCHIST'S ALMANAC

MIKE HARDING

Illustrated by Bill Tidy

ANAC

ARROW BOOKS

Arrow Books Limited
17–21 Conway Street, London W1P 6JD

An imprint of the Hutchinson Publishing Group

London Melbourne Sydney Auckland
Johannesburg and agencies throughout
the world

First published by Robson Books Ltd 1981
Arrow edition 1982
Reprinted 1982

Set in Linotron Plantin by
Rowland Phototypesetting Ltd
Bury St Edmunds, Suffolk

Made and printed in Great Britain
by The Anchor Press Ltd
Tiptree, Essex

ISBN 0 09 929210 6

How to survive almost everything,
without doing anything very much, from
the comfort of your own armchair.
A complete field manual for the urbane
guerrilla, in alphabetical order, from
Aardvark to Zylophone.*

Tired of living? Feared of dying?

Don't want to tote that bale of cotton?

Worried about mortgages, insurance, school, dandruff, the meaning of life, falling hair, quasi-stellar galaxies, the damp patch on the ceiling?

Do you ever wonder if it's all a plot?

Do you ever want to say 'no' to everything?

Do you think that red-headed women make better lovers? And if so . . . than what?

Do you think the world could be flat after all? . . .

THEN THIS BOOK
IS FOR YOU !!!!!

**The first book
that tells you...
what it's all about - ?**

- **How to pull a hat out of a rabbit**

- **How God got the job**

- **How to hypnotize stones**

● Who slept with whom...famous historical legovers

● What to do if the bomb drops

● What to do if it doesn't drop

This is the fun, fun, fun personal battery-powered book, especially made with paper fetishists in mind. Enjoy it in the secrecy of your own home.

THIS BOOK IS ENVIRONMENTALLY POSITIVE ...

It will burn, wipe things up, and can be used as a pillow, a breeding cage for dormice or as a filing system for your pancakes. It can be used to steady a table with one leg shorter than the other three or three legs longer than the other one. It can be used for hammering worms back into the soil, for keeping apart charging wooden elephants and pressing very small pairs of trousers.

Designed with the Armchair Anarchist in mind – who gets impatient at having to plough through acres of highly stylized verbiage to get at whatever the getter-at's getting at – this book is an almanac. You can scan it, dip into it, leave it lying about to impress your friends, consult it in an emergency, and quote from it without fear of any contradiction since everything written within these covers is the last word on the subject, and that's final . . . I think.

INTRODUCTION

The Concise Oxford Dictionary defines Anarchy as 'Absence of government; disorder; confusion' and defines an Anarchist as an 'advocate of Anarchy'.

As Her Royal Highness Queen Victoria once said on looking up her gillie's kilt, 'What a load of cobblers!' Defining an Anarchist in those terms is like saying that a fireman is an advocate of burning buildings, a doctor is an advocate of children with dried peas stuck up their nostrils or a policeman is an advocate of little men with masks, striped jerseys and bags with SWAG written on them.

True Anarchists do not advocate Anarchy any more than astronomers advocate black dwarfs. The old image of an Anarchist as a black-caped, black-hearted crusader complete with stove pipe hat and little black bomb is one that went out with Film Fun, gob-stoppers, Dick Barton and suspenders for men.

Anarchists do not encourage or assist or promulgate or in any way stimulate disorder and confusion – they just recognize the fact that all about them confusion and disorder reign. As Virgil says in his Eclogues

Omnes Vita unus sublimus chanticlerus est,

('Life is one great Cock Up') and who are we to argue with him? Particularly since he's dead and in any case his dad's bigger than yours.

Medical research has recently unearthed a tiny organ, invisible to the naked medical researcher with an electron microscope and only, in fact, visible after three Hail Mary's and a perfect act of foolishness. This organ, according to reports in the March 1979 issue of the *Neurosurgeons' and Fish Fryers' Monthly*, is a small but important gland situated somewhere between the cerebral cortex and the bits you enjoy washing most of all.

It is believed that it is this gland which the ancient dipsticks called the 'Astral Mirror' or 'Third Eye'. It is this gland that the Holy Men of India speak of when they call upon 'the eye within that sees the heavenly light of Shiva that streams through the universe'. It is this gland that enables Tibetan monks to remain motionless naked in the snow for nineteen years; it is this gland that gave Shelly, Byron and Keats the insight into Man that brought out their finest poetry; and it is this gland that makes you fart after leek soup and sherry trifle.

Without this gland Coleridge would never have written *The Ancient Mariner*, but there again without this gland the mariner might not have been stupid enough to shoot the albatross in the first place.

' 'Tis all a checkerboard of nights and days,' said Omar Khayyam. But for a long time nobody listened to him, asking themselves (and who can blame them?), 'What does a carpet fitter and battered caravanserai repairer know about astro-physics? If he's that clever why doesn't he tell us what's going to win the 3.30 tomorrow at York?' The same question has since been levelled at many of the great thinkers of our time. (Bertrand Russell did in fact predict the winner of the first two races at Doncaster but his third choice went down at Aintree. Einstein was no good on horses but made a bit on the dogs while Leonardo Da Vinci was said to have been red hot on which fly would land on a cube of sugar first.)

The name the scientists have given to this perceptual gland is the Bugadifino gland after its discoverer, Roger. This is the gland that when, on a cloudless starry night, you look at the vast, fiery citadels falling back cluster after cluster into the dark nothingness of eternity and ask in an awed voice, 'What's it all about?' answers, 'Bugadifino pal, Bugadifino.'

In Anarchists the Bugadifino gland is usually the most advanced of all the organs of the body. The Bugadifino gland is also the one gland of the body that strengthens most with usage. Let me give you an example . . . .

It is Monday morning; the time 8.08. The roads to the city are clogged with traffic. Thousands of cars, are inching bumper to bumper towards the smoky metropolis like immense skeins of gigantic poppet beads. The tailbacks stringing down the urban clearways are several miles long. All over the world, in every major city from Rio to Bombay, Cairo to Leeds, cars are moving at the exact rate of 13.5 m.p.h. The whole world is going to be late for work.

In millions of cars ulcers are popping as gastric juices swill round mixtures of Super Yummy Brecky Flakes, freeze-dried coffee, Mother Hubbard's soggy, steamed, bleached and preservative-stuffed bread and artificially constituted Honey Bunched Syrup Spread. The whole lot is turning into a mixture so lethal it could eat through a second-hand car salesman's heart in 2.8 secs. In millions of cars lips are sucking on nicotine-flavoured nipple substitutes, and ears are assaulted by the manic gibberish of disc jockeys whose cerebral power wouldn't equip them to engage a chimpanzee in a game of snap.

In one car sits Eric Massman, symbol of the world's little men. His radio is on.

'And a special hello to all you people out there stuck on the clearways. This is Rockin' Ronnie here and on the turntable is a new disc from the Smegmas – it's their latest release, a song called *I Never Wanted to be Born Anyway. With a Bit of Luck I could have Ended up on the Bedroom Ceiling*. So here we go . . .

Little Eric Massman sits in the centre of a sea of cars in his five-year-old banger that he hasn't a hope of replacing, with 2.4 children, a wife, a mortgage and a leaking toilet back at home. Little Eric Massman is eating what is left of his nails, glancing all the while at his cheap digital watch, running his fingers through his hair feeling for the beginnings of a bald patch, feeling his stomach to see if he's getting a paunch (he is), tapping his feet on the pedals, revving up more fumes out into the muggy lead-filled, early summer morning air.

'Why do we do it?' he asks himself.

'Bugadifino,' says a small voice at the back of his brain.

'What's the point of it all?' he cries.

'Bugadifino,' comes the answer again.

'We must be mad doing this day after day, pouring into the offices and factories to make a load of junk so that other stupid Herberts who go into other offices and factories can buy our junk and we can buy theirs and so it goes on week in, week out, the same bloody thing tomorrow and tomorrow and the day after until we bloody die and what for? WHY? WHY? WHY? THAT'S WHAT I WANT TO KNOW!' He screams half demented, not conscious of the faces looking curiously at him from the other cars.

And the little gland inside his head just answers, 'Bugadifino, pal, Bugadifino.'

The realization that he can do nothing at all about the Great Roller Coaster of Life* except get off it produces within Eric Massman a stimulation of the Bugadifino gland to danger-point – for it leads him on to more doubt and more questions to which the only answer is more 'Bugadifinos'.

He gets to work, works all day at the same brain-softening job, goes home through the same traffic jam listening to the disc jockey's brother playing a record called *I Got Pregnant at Butlins* by Lusty Lizzie and the Plastic Dolls. He has a tea that consists largely of frozen chips made from reconstituted potatoes, some monosodium glutamate and formaldehyde held together with some stringy bits of what was once a cow and some pale sprouts that last saw the light of day six years before in a Czechoslovakian field. After tea he sits down to a cup of tea dust and an indigestion tablet and watches a situation comedy on the television. The plot is very simple – two people are trying to write a plot for a situation comedy about two people writing a situation comedy set in the operating theatre of a spare-part transplant hospital called *Bits and Pieces*. He gets up and has a wash and goes to a mock-Elizabethan pub on the edge of the estate where he sits drinking chemical pasteurized fizz and eating indiges-

*Atheism and the Art of Push Bike Peddling Arthur Grimsdyke.

tion tablets to the accompaniment of 'muzak in the night' until it's time to go home.

All the while his mind is asking 'Why?' and a little voice is saying 'Bugadifino'. He stands before his two-year-old mortgage commitment looking at the garage doors hanging off in the moonlight, the newspaper stuffed in the cracks between the window frames and the wall to keep the draught out, the tiles that have avalanched into the gutter from the warped roof, the overflow that is dripping from the cistern in the loft. He goes in and, as he's looking up at the brown patch on the ceiling caused by the leaking toilet, he slips on a dayglow puppet frog that one of the kids has left on the tiled kitchen floor.

As he lies in agony with a twisted back and severe damage to the smile muscles, a little voice, unprompted, mutters:

'Bugadifino, pal, Bugadifino.'

HOW TO BE AN ANARCHIST FROM THE SAFETY OF YOUR OWN ARMCHAIR AND IN THE PRIVACY OF YOUR OWN HOME

Have you the makings of an armchair anarchist?

1 Recognize the fact that the Cosmos has it in for you personally and you are already scoring 57 points out of 100 on the Whymeometer.

2 Some people are born good looking, talented, rich, capable, confident, bursting with health . . . these people don't need almanacs, they need ground glass sandwiches, belladonna tea and a job in a Barbara Cartland novel. If you are not amongst the earthborn gods that dominate the William Hickey column and the Sunday shiny comics then award yourself a further 13 points.

3 If you answer yes to any three of the following questions, award yourself a further 30 points. If you answer yes to more than three you should be writing this book yourself.

QUIZ

1 Has the cork ever broken in the wine bottle as you were trying to open it?
2 Has an acquaintance that you don't much like ever given you his baby to hold and it's peed on you?
3 Do drunks on buses always talk to you rather than anybody else?
4 Do you have trouble getting chairs through doorways?
5 Do you think vests are silly?
6 Does your mind ever wander while you're making love?
7 Do you hate people who put overcoats on dogs?
8 Do you think most politicians are
   (a) stupid?
   (b) crooks?
   (c) both?
9 Have you ever wished that God would come out into the open and own up?
10 Have you ever wanted the baddies in a film to win?
11 Have you ever wondered why women cover up their knees when they're wearing skirts and yet don't mind showing all their legs when they're wearing shorts?
12 Have you ever wanted to strangle a disc jockey?
13 Have you ever
   (a) dreamed that you murdered your boss?
   (b) cried when you realized it was only a dream?
14 Have you ever, on a dark night alone in an old house, had the feeling that perhaps there might be ghosts after all?
15 Have you ever felt like laughing at a funeral?
16 Have you ever wanted to get hold of some of the people who make television commercials and hit them?

17 Do you sometimes think God is a heavy drinker?

18 Do you feel guilty when a policeman talks to you even though you have done nothing wrong?

19 Have you ever lain awake worrying about a library book you should have taken back?

20 Have you ever dreamed that you saved the life of someone you had a crush on and they fell in love with you?

21 When you were a child, did you ever wonder if your teacher went to the toilet?

22 Did you ever have nightmares about going to school dressed only in a vest that was too short anyway?

23 Have you ever looked at a work of modern art and wondered if the artist is
(a) taking the mickey?
(b) totally potty?

24 Have you realized that if there were no governments there would be no wars?

25 Have you ever wanted to shout rude things in a public place?

26 Have you ever wished you were God?

SOME
WARM-UP
EXERCISES IN
ARMCHAIR
ANARCHY

Having read so far, you should have found out whether or not you have the makings of an Armchair Anarchist. If you have, then all well and good – carry on reading the rest of the book. If you haven't then take this book back to the bookshop and exchange it for 17 Barbara Cartland novels, 26 Enid Blytons or a book on tropical mushroom cultivation since you obviously believe, like Pippa, that 'God's in His Heaven, all's right with the world'.

If you've decided to 'stick with it concept-wise', as Henry Ford once said, then

1 find a good armchair;
2 rehearse the key phrases of your new mantra – 'It's all a load of rubbish', 'They're all mad except me and I', 'They're all in it together';
3 curl up in the foetal position;
4 expect the worse.

Suspect everything. Experience will teach you that things are either true, or the work of the CIA or in the *Daily Telegraph*. Let me state categorically that this is not the work of the CIA or the *Daily Telegraph* and most of it is true, or nearly, unless it is a mistake, of course . . . Honest.

AARDVARKS

Aardvarks are laughing people from the town of Grottstadt in Holland. They were originally created as a guild of
laughing craftsmen by a medieval friar called Läftilit
Hertz. Aardvarks are usually employed as plants by poor
cabaret comedians. Their craft is passed on from father to
son and the secrets of their trade are jealously guarded.
They were regularly employed in Britain by 'Follow That'
Smith and Eric 'Coffin Jokes' Doomsby, two of Europe's
worst comedians.

The Aardvarks are believed to trace their craft back to
the Fenestration of Grottstadt when people who failed to
laugh at the jokes of the invading Huns were thrown into
houses through the windows. The formation of the guild
of Master Laughers was bitterly opposed by the guild of
Master Glazers and effigies of Laftilit Hertz were hit with
soused herrings in the streets of Grottstadt.

Each year Aardvarks are shipped in vast numbers to
Britain for the Royal Variety Command Performance.
Many a poor comedian on leaving the stage to the sound of
his own footsteps and one laugh has been heard to remark
'That was Aardvark'.

The fact that the crime of murder is unknown in
Grottstadt led to the saying 'Aardvark never killed anybody'.

ACCIDENTS _____

Accidents cause History.

If Sigismund Unbuckle had not taken a walk in 1426 and met Wat Tyler, the Peasants' Revolt would never have happened and the motor car would not have been invented until 2026, which would have meant that all the oil could have been used for lamps thus saving the electric light bulb and the whale and nobody would have caught Moby Dick or Billy Budd.

ADOLESCENCE _____

A period of growing pains, growing period pains and general spottiness. Boys have smelly feet and armpits at this stage; girls slam doors and dream. If you're going through it, hard luck. If you're a parent and going through it with them:

1 Try and remember what it was like, e.g. clothes didn't fit; everybody laughed at you; you had to shave/buy a bra for the first time.
2 Resign yourself to underarm hairs in the razor, spot cream everywhere, doors hanging off, and their appalling friends lounging all over your chairs drinking all your coffee.

But always remember that you did it, too.

AEROPLANES

If God had meant us to fly, he'd have given us turbo props
THE ARCHBISHOP OF BARNSLEY

The first aeroplane was invented by Jim Gropespierre of Lower Bendover in Kent in 1809.

Gropespierre spent much of his youth and childhood observing crows landing in the fields while working as a bird scarer. He spent so much time watching instead of scaring that he got the sack but not before becoming an expert on their habits. He noticed, for instance, that the birds' diet consisted in the main of small insects, the heads of young corn and dead things. By simple deduction Gropespierre came to the conclusion that the same diet would enable man to fly. He lived for ten years on earwigs, bird seed and *The Times* obituary columns, until his payload on take off was 6lbs 7ozs.

With wings fashioned from old copies of the *Boys' Own Paper* and *Health and Efficiency*, he launched himself from the top of Wormby Cliffs under the watchful gaze of four cows and a reporter from the *Wormby Sentinel*. He plummeted 400 feet before hitting a hot thermal which gripped the wings of his primitive etherboat *The Atmosclipper* and sent him 700 feet into the air. He was carried inland for several hundred miles before being shot by a deranged stone-breaker at Beckenham. Thinking a large pond he had just crossed was the Channel, he addressed the stone-breaker (who was a deaf-mute) in gabbled *Français*.

'*Je suis l'homme première volant,*' he shouted boldly.

The man felled him with his hammer and led him to the nearest village where, on regaining consciousness, he proceeded to address everybody in French. He was in-

stantly hanged as a spy, thus becoming the first casualty of air travel.

Since Gropespierre's day, the aeroplane has become a widely accepted form of transport (see *Air Travel*). If forced to travel on an aeroplane, try and get in the cabin with the Captain, so you can keep an eye on him and nudge him if he falls asleep or point out any mountains looming up ahead.

He's only human after all.

AIR TRAVEL _____

Once you've decided that you're going, the quickest – though by no means the safest – means of travel is via the big silver sparrow.

The problems the Armchair Anarchist has to face are not connected with the flight. The only worries are

1 What's that noise?
2 Why is the Stewardess crying?
3 Is the Captain a crazed madman?
4 Why is that wing shaking?
5 Why did the Captain need that white stick to get on the plane?
6 Why is my lucky rabbit's foot walking unassisted off the plane?
7 Why are we landing in Cuba?

These are just a few of the worries you are sure to have during the flight. Face facts, there is nothing you can do then except hope and pray that Leonardo's scribbles weren't too far out or that metal fowlpest is a figment of a sick humorist's imagination.

The real problems are found getting to and from the plane.

1 You're loaded down with luggage;
2 The check-in is *always* at least 7 miles from the car park.
   So you'll have to walk. There will be a train of luggage
   trolleys chained together but no one will have the key to
   the lock. Instead porters will offer to carry your bags for
   tips that make Dick Turpin look like little Lord Fauntleroy.

What can you do?

Don't take baggage. The average holidaymaker carries
enough kit with him to provision Mungo Park's travels:

   3 complete evening outfits
   16 changes of underwear
   That 'sporty' shirt Aunty Thingy gave him and he never
   dared wear in the garden
   4 swimming costumes
   6 ties
   4 pairs of shoes
   1 pair of sandals
   3 pairs slacks/dresses (6)
   Another 6 shirts/blouses

Bag containing sun tan oil, burning lotion, stomach
pills, headache tablets, sickness and diarrhoea tablets,
safety pins, plasters, shaving tackle, contraceptives,
Uncle Harry's Burma Railway shorts, two cameras,
eleven biros and 2 funny hats from Blackpool.

Take one set of clothes and the contraceptives and you
can leave the rest.

If you're going to need all that skin care and diarrhoea
stuff you shouldn't go in the first place – go to an Ill Health
Farm where hypochondriacs can hobble in the damp
bronchial fens of the border marshes and where a whole
hour of every day is devoted to sitting on lavatory seats in
the hope of catching something.

Otherwise, if you're going on holiday in the sun you'll be spending all your time by the pool or in the bar so – *you won't need all that gear!*

One set of underwear is enough if you beat it with a stick every night and stand clear of magnetic instruments. Stay out of the sun and laugh at all the sandblasted people hopping to hospital along the hot tarmac to the hysterical hoots of the Spaniards/Maltese/Greeks.

So you've left all the gear behind. You walk out of the car carrying a Woolworth's carrier bag, promenade past powerless and furious porters and try and find the check-in desk.

Face facts. If they made flying dead easy they wouldn't be able to charge so much for it. The girl behind the counter, when you eventually find it

1 Hates the stupid uniform with the Tyrolean hat, Irish Shamrock and Jamaican bananas that she has to wear as a result of an amalgamation between Swiss, West Indian Airlines and Aer Limerick.
2 Her fiancé/husband/lover has run away with a beautiful schoolgirl that morning.
3 Her feet are throbbing.
4 Her dog got ran over that morning.
5 She's got a hangover/earache/toothache.
6 She's not going on holiday and you are.
7 She's just dealt with eleven hundred lost Japanese.

Add all this up and you can see she's not going to help you much.

Hand over the tickets, smile and DON'T LET HER PUT A LABEL ON ANYTHING – it will end up in Reykjavik which is OK if you're one of the 27 people a year who go there.

Some general hints

Watch out for a small, grey-haired woman with rhinestone glasses and a Brooklyn accent, two luggage trolleys and 24 suitcases. If you look at her and she catches your eye, she will follow you all over the airport asking questions and you'll be stuck with her for ever. She's the modern-day equivalent of the Old Man of the Sea.

Try not to shoot any albatrosses from the plane window or the rest of the flight may be manned by a skeleton crew.

Don't smile at any Serbo Croats leaning against the duty-free sign or bookstall. This will be construed as an invitation to marry their sisters and run a Maluck stall in Irkoventsk.

AKIMBO, LEGS _____

'Legs' Akimbo was a hit man for the Barnsley Mafia in the 1930s until he was lured from the path of crime by a Salvation Army girl in 1936. After a pitched battle with the Salvation Army Provisionals outside the 'Canary and Lunatic Dentist' public house in Barnsley's Lower East Side, Legs Akimbo was wounded by a fragment from a Holy Water Bottle and was nursed back to health by Vera Religious, a bandage winder for the Sunbeam Sappers. The battle for control of the pitch and toss sites and sasparella stills was eventually won by the Provos in 1937.

In the autumn of that year Akimbo and Vera were married and Akimbo founded the West Riding Junior Anarchist League with Renee Pickles, Fish Jim, Bob Nazel Spray and Jock the Coalman. The organization never met, had no manifesto, no officers, no offices and (since all the members resigned the same day on the grounds that it was getting too organized) no membership.

AMERICA _____

America was discovered by Amerigo Vespucci and named after him, until people got tired of living in a place called Vespuccia and changed its name to America.

Had the first captain to sail those waters discovered it, America could have ended up being called 'Bert' after Captain Hookfoot Bert, Pirate, Buccaneer and one time Whitby deckchair attendant. Bert, however, took a wrong

turning at Barrow-in-Furness and instead discovered King's Lynn, which was a bit of a waste of time because most people knew it was there anyway.

Mind you, had Vespucci discovered King's Lynn it would be America now which would be unfortunate since Ronald Reagan would have to declare war on Russia with a population the size of an average block of council flats in Moscow, all of which goes to show etc. etc.

46

ANGST

Angst is something every home should have, an unidentifiable feeling of overburdening guilt that seems to have little cause or reason. It's usually something to do with overbearing mothers, a Roman Catholic upbringing, grubby underwear or overdue library books. If you've got the lot then you've had it.

The measure of angst is the angstrom. Poets (e.g. Shelley, Heine, McGonagall) have 10 to 14 angstrom on a scale with a 15 maximum. Designers of maternity brassières and novelty cigars usually register 0.4 while the lowest recorded reading on an angstrometer is 0.1 scored by garden snails and right-wing politicians.

ANIMALS

There's a good Cyclops ODYSSEUS
I'm just taking the Minotaur for a walk, dear THESEUS
Dad! Caliban's done it on the carpet again! MIRANDA.

Since Man crawled blinking out of the mud and began to climb trees he has mistakenly assumed that the special relationship he thinks he has with God entitles him to regard the animals who share his planet with him as inferior beings to be beaten, eaten, pampered, kicked, laughed at, tortured and worked to death.

'You act like an animal' is in a way a strange sort of compliment if by that you mean any animal other than

Man. For what other animal has murdered, bombed, napalmed, raped, assassinated, gassed, exterminated and regularly enslaved his own kind since the beginnings of Time? What Man fails to realize is that through his own stupidity Man is bringing about his own extinction as well as that of all the other animals on this planet.

Animals other than Man tend to be better behaved. They don't get drunk, beat each other up at football matches or take photographs of each other with no fur on. They don't need Popes, Bishops, Prime Ministers or Kings to teach them how to behave and, probably most important of all, they don't use money.

ANIMALS, DANGEROUS

The most dangerous animals to Man (after Man himself) are those that can either fall on you and squash you, bite you, sting you or make you sneeze so much you swallow your false teeth and choke to death.

Some points to remember

1 Don't go to sleep under big animals, e.g. elephants, rhinoceri, hippopotamuses;
2 Don't put animals with sharp teeth or poisonous fangs down the front of your clothes (look what happened to Cleopatra);
3 Don't pat certain animals, e.g. crocodiles and scorpions or dogs you have just kicked.

On the whole, animals and men would get along together much better apart – particularly the last seventy otters left in England.

ANIMALS, REALLY DANGEROUS

The Gnurd

The Gnurd lives on wax paper cups and soup stains and has been known to attack Vendomatic engineers and school dinner ladies without provocation. Often seen lurking round motorway service cafés.

DAD RAN OVER IT ON THE M6 BUT IT SEEMS BETTER NOW!

The Psblurtex

The Psblurtex is an 18-inch long anaconda that hides in the gentlemen's outfitting departments of Amazonian stores and is often bought by mistake since its colours are those of the London Reform Club. Once tied around its victim's neck, it strangles him gently and then claims the insurance before running off to Germany where it lives in hiding.

APHRODISIACS _____

Not oysters again BLUEBEARD

I'll be glad when there's an R in the month THE MRS SOLOMONS

Cherries and whipped cream
Nowadays, even quite respectable cake shops sell cherries and whipped cream. These were once only available from Paris or certain postal houses in the south of England and had to be sent through the post in a sealed plain envelope.

Celery
Celery is an ancient aphrodisiac well known to the Aztecs who used it as a splint.

Electrical gadgets
These are all well and good but, if you want to make love on a romantic beach, in the moonlight, you're going to have to run out a hell of a lot of cable and could stand the chance of a bad earth loop, or even wow and flutter or,

perhaps worst of all, a short across some of your points resulting in a burn-out or, at the very least, interference on televisions for miles around.

Ladders
Handy for the undersized male.

Powdered rhinoceros horn
This has been cited as stimulating the sex drive. It may do, but it can have side-effects. After too much rhino horn, you might want to go out and ram a Landrover.

Washing machines
Washing machines give you more time to do it and less time banging your vest between a couple of rocks in a cold river.

Whips, leather masks, dog-collars, pencil-sharpeners etc.
Whips and masks are all right in their own way, but remember they take a long time to put on and by the time you've got into all the gear you could have forgotten what you were doing in the first place. Even worse, if there's a fire and you run out into the street in your gear, you could be mistaken for Spiderman or the Lone Ranger and be expected to put the fire out.

APOCALYPSE _____

If you see four horsemen coming towards you –

1 phone the fire brigade
2 remove any sharp objects from your pockets
3 run

ARCHITECTS _____

We've made too many doorways, Murphy CARACATUS
O'RIORDAN, BUILDER STONEHENGE. ARCHITECTS COGI-
DUMNUS POULSON AND CO.

Architects are people who don't like fields SMALL BOY

The very first architect was Eric Gog of the Neanderthalers who leant his spear against a rock and threw his cloak
over it while he went to look at the solstice. When he came
back it had been rented off to a family of 16 and there was
smoke coming out of the armholes.

For the rest of his life Gog went round leaning spears and cloaks against rocks and things and renting them off. He called these cloakrooms. He was stoned to death when his first multi-storey block collapsed when a drunk took one of the bottom poles away to hit his dog with.

Eric's son Goose took over the business and made a fortune selling plans of his invention to other Neanderthalers. Since then, most buildings have been designed by architects, some of them good, most of them diabolical. Just go to any city and look.

The Pisa police are still looking for the man who designed the leaning tower. He is believed to be a one-eyed illiterate Lascar who later went on to design the first underground airport.

ARISTOCRACY _____

The English aristocracy are, without any doubt, the best criminals in the world since for hundreds of years they have been exploiting and robbing the people of this country and any other they have landed in. Not only have they managed to get away with it, they have also been given peerages for doing it, not to mention weekly appearances in the blue press and jobs on the boards of major companies.

How to wipe out the aristocracy

Don't let your daughters or sons marry any of them and their inbreeding will cause genetic mutations until they die out or, like George III, hop about the room thinking that they're frogs.

ARMY _____

If you like travel, adventure, seeing foreign countries, meeting the natives, learning their language and killing them, then the Army is the place for you. The only drawback is that you might get hurt in the process.

At one time armies were a sort of kings' hobby. The king would build up an army and find some sort of grievance with another king that would result in a war. They'd campaign during the summer (days only), mark their positions, and then pack up and go home when the first frost appeared on their halberds and ballistas. Next spring they'd all be back in their positions knocking seven lumps of good for the roses off each other. It was unthinkable that anyone would hit a knight who had fallen off his horse, much less pour hot tar on his stumps, although it was not unknown for knights to be weighed in as scrap.

With the arrival of sponsorship in the game (nationalism, vested interests, territorial designs etc.) things started to get tough. People started hitting knights on the ground, putting stones in their snowballs and pouring the contents of the chip pan out of the dormer windows on to the rent man. People also started fighting wars for the most stupid causes: religion, women, the annexation of the Saar and the Polish Corridor (although everybody knew it was damp and let rain in) and the Ukrainian Back Passage. The craziest war ever was the War of Jenkins's Ear since there was nobody else it would fit.

Most of the people who got hurt in those early wars were the commoners, the fatality rate for kings was pretty damn low. In fact, if you were going to go to war, the best thing to be was a king since the chances were that you wouldn't be killed until last, if at all, as the usual punishment for kings who had cocked it up and lost was banishment to an island somewhere. Usually it was the little men on both sides who copped it, a situation that hasn't changed to this day and if the little men of the world would only realize then the warmongering kings and politicians of the world will have to put on boxing gloves and go and knock seven lumps of good for the roses out of each other with no back-up team. Mind you, there'll probably always be some sneak who'll creep up and grab onto the coat tails of power saying something like, 'I'll give you a hand if you give me Yorkshire when you win.'

Has it ever occurred to anyone that yesterday's enemies nearly always end up as today's trading partners? England has fought wars with the French, Germans, Spanish, Belgians, Dutch and Americans at some time or another. We are now on chummy terms with all of them – eat their food, drink their wine and go there to get sunburn and the trotters.

ATOM BOMB

The Russians are terrified of using it, the Americans don't want to use it because they've just decorated, the Chinese are too clever to use it, the Irish can't remember where they've put it and the English would have to fill too many forms in to use it. If the Scots get it, don't go to Glasgow on a Saturday night.
ERIC DOPPLEGANGER, 'A Plain Man's Guide to World War Three'.

Most people are frightened of the atom bomb and I personally would cross the road if I saw one coming; in fact most people are now of the opinion that Mr and Mrs Einstein should never have given little Albert that chemistry set in the first place.

If an atom bomb lands near you or if the dog brings one in from the garden –

1 don't touch it
2 phone the fire brigade
3 run

If an atom bomb goes off near you –

1 put your fingers in your ears
2 wait till the bang is over
3 count all your bits – arms, legs, shopping bags etc.
4 phone the fire brigade
5 run
6 don't kiss anyone who's radioactive or use a toilet seat after they've been in there.

After the apocalypse, the idiots who started it all will emerge from holes in the ground and try and organize all the rubble and dust into little piles so that they can fight over them again. A well-aimed brick or colour television should send them back in their holes for a bit.

BABIES

Honest dad I found him in the bullrushes MISS PHAROAH

Ma he's making eye at me BABY CYCLOPS

Go on then have a baby
If you really must
Babies are better than rabies
But only just
OGDEN GNASH

Babies are loud and dangerous at both ends and should ideally be approached from the middle . . . if at all.

They tend to be orally fixated and will go for anything hanging so beware of leaning over prams with pipes/glasses/ball-point pens/lucky charms/long neckties or piccolos as the baby will eat them. If this happens there will be nothing you can do since babies are not criminally liable until they are 14 months old.

Babies are usually terribly ugly. However, Nature has seen to it that their mothers are totally blind to this fact and think them really beautiful, a biological phenomenon that has ensured the continuation of the species.

If you are shown a baby, gurgle and coo and say things like 'Oooza biggie liddle iddsy yummy dingy wingey'. I know it sounds ridiculous but babies and mothers like this sort of thing.

Guess its weight at least three to four pounds heavier than you think it is. Mothers like to think that their babies are fat, another puzzling feature.

Whatever you do, try not to hold it or it will almost certainly throw up on you. Babies are like dogs, they can smell fear a mile off but since they can't bite you yet, they

58

either pee on you or cover your best suede jacket with a mixture of dribble and recycled vegetable and prune puree. If there is no way you can avoid holding a baby (e.g. if it is yours) most Army and Navy stores sell complete suits of heavy duty arctic fishermen's oilskins, including sou'westers.

If you are forced to change the baby's nappy, remember that you pin the baby's nappy to its vest not its skin. For nappy changing Army and Navy stores also sell gauntlets and chemical warfare masks.

If baby cries too much, a small cigar and a couple of large whiskies should help him to sleep.

BARBERS _____

I wish he'd shut up singing and come and cut my bloody hair
HAIRY PERSON OF SEVILLE.

The most famous barbers of all time were Mrs Samson and Sweeney Todd. They still serve as an example of what the worst barbers can get up to.

In the days when I used to go to the barber's as a kid, a red and white pole stuck out rampant above the grimy shop and the sign FOUR ASSISTANTS NO WAITING meant that ten minutes after going in you staggered out like a hedge-hog that had come off badly in a fight with a shearing machine. Small boys were sat on boards placed across the arms of the chair and while talking to you the barber would lean over and tell jokes to coughing men at the other side of the shop, sell rubber goods to furtive young men who glided in and out like shadows and pocket bets from more furtive older men who shambled in looking airily around as though the last thing in the world they had on their minds was what was going to win the 3.30 at Haydock. In the days before betting on horses was legalized, the barber I went to was jam packed from morning to early evening and the barber cut about four heads a day. If you wanted a haircut you had to nip in after the racing had finished.

I think it's a shame that people today, men and women, don't shave their heads and wear wigs or paint them funny colours. It would be an accurate indication of a person's moods that day, in the same way that the colours on a baboon's bum can tell you whether it wants to fight or make love. The vanity of fashion is robbing us of yet another form of signals and communication.

A word of advice regarding barbers –

> don't go to any barber with a pie shop next door;
> don't let your wife cut your hair if you've got a temple to push down the next day.

BARNSLEY

The people of Barnsley have threatened to kill Fred Willis of Glamorgan if he ever goes there. Fred Willis says he has no intention of going there. The affair continues in this state of tension.

BARROW-IN-FURNESS

Barrow-in-Furness has more people with webbed feet than any other British town.

BECKENHAM, SIDNEY

Sidney Beckenham of Basildon was a British patriot of such fervour that he had all his clothes made from Union Jacks and had his face and hands tattooed like Union Jacks as well. He was twice flown at half mast by mistake and on a sea-cruise fell asleep in a deck-chair. The purser, thinking he was a flag-draped corpse, had him tipped over the side into the sea where he drowned.

BERKINS, JAS _____

Jas Berkins of Salford tried to eat himself for a bet, but died from shock while still on his right foot, thus forfeiting the prize, a year's supply of *The Poultry Breeders' Weekly News*.

BIBLE, THE _____

Most Armchair Anarchists know that the Bible consists of a large number of separate books, some of which are apocryphal and some of which aren't all that bad.

The Bible as we know is, in fact, a corruption of an earlier set of books, the Books of Eric. The original manuscripts of the Books of Eric were found recently in a cave high on the moors above Hardcastle Crags. Eric, unlike the Jaweh of the Jews, is human and fallible. In fact, he's more like the God we experience in our daily lives rather than the Sunday one. In fact, he's a right dozy pratt.

The following is an excerpt from the Books of Eric.

In the beginning was the Word, and the Word was Eric.

And there was all about a great nothingness, a void.

And along came Eric and he did cock it up. He took the earth that was above and the waters that were below and made of them mud. And that was the first day.

And there was still a great darkness over the face of the Earth and Eric cried, 'Let there be light!' and nothing happened. And Eric wandered round in the dark bumping into things crying, 'Let there be light! Let there be bleedin' light!' And on the second day he found the switch and there was light and it did fuse the Milky Way.

And on the third day Eric overslept and woke late crying, 'Let there be grass and trees and fruit thereof!' And lo, it came to pass. But they were under the sea, for Eric had forgotten to say where. And it took him the rest of the third day to sort it out.

And on the fourth day Eric said, 'What the Hell's a day?' and so he should know the light from the dark he invented the alarm clock and tea-time and muffins and pyjamas. And that was on the fourth day.

Then Eric said, 'Let the waters bring forth moving creatures that hath life and fowl that may fly in the heavens and creatures that may walk on the face of the earth.' And it was so. And there did come forth many creatures and they began to eat each other and the fowls of the air did drop dung on the head of Eric and the beasts did do it on

his carpet. And the evening and the morning were the fifth day.

On the sixth day Eric said, 'Let us make a Man in our own image and likeness and let him have dominion over the fish of the sea and over the fowl of the air and over the cattle and over every creeping thing on the earth.' So Eric made man in his own image and in his own likeness and

Man fell over. And the stinging nettles stung him and the creeping things did bite him and he did find it impossible to get chairs through doorways without banging his shins and trapping his fingers and the fowl of the air did drop dung on his head and that was the sixth day.

And on the seventh day Eric washed his car and took the dog to the park.

And Eric did make a garden for the Man and it was called Eden and in it there were all the herbs of the field and all the animals that were good. And Eric said to the man, 'Of all the trees in the garden mayest thou eat save the tree wherein is hidden the foolishness of Eric and the cock-ups he has made! Also mayest thou not park thy car before my drive nor lettest thy dog dig up my roses.' And it came to pass.

And Eric said, 'It is not good that Man should be lonely: I will make an helpmeet for him.'

And while the Man did sleep Eric did open his side and did take out thereof a rib. And lo! the man died. And Eric had to begin all over again.

BIRMINGHAM

I've nothing against the people of Birmingham at all, I just think that their city is one of the ugliest in the world and has proved the theory that the motor car has done more to destroy the cities of Britain than two world wars (not to mention crooked councillors and bent architects). Unfortunately, most other cities in Britain are getting to look like Birmingham, including Manchester which now has the largest tiled urinal in the world in the shape of the Arndale Centre. Apparently the man who designed this ceramic abortion was savaged to death by his guide dog.

BOLTON _____

The people of Bolton walk backwards whenever they see a midget. After Bertram Mills Circus appeared there in 1927, half the population walked backwards into the river and drowned.

BREAST
FEEDING _____

This should not be attempted by fathers with hairy chests since they can make the baby sneeze and give it wind.

Do not do it on a train unless you know everybody on it or they may think you are being eaten by a cannibal for a circus midget liberation guerilla movement and pull the excommunication cord.

Don't breast feed baby after his eighteenth year as this only makes parting harder and his friends at the disco will laugh at him.

Feeding through the school railings at play-time can give baby lines on his forehead.

CHESTERFIELD _____

Chesterfield was visited with a plague of laughing in 1936 that lasted for three months. Since then no comic has ever raised a laugh in Chesterfield.

CITIES _____

Cities were organic things at one time. People would cross a river at a certain point and build a bridge. Then a few houses and a pub would get put up, then a cobbler's and a blacksmith's and an abbey and a swimming baths and a town hall and a bank and a grammar school and a cinema and a hospital and some tea rooms and a few more pubs and a library and, as people needed things, so they added them.

Cities had interesting corners and little gardens and shops that sold hot muffins or made very good coffee or could be guaranteed to have the very book in that you were looking for. If you wanted a pair of leather boot laces or some snuff or a Rolls-Royce, there was usually somewhere in a city that you could get them.

Then along came the town planner.

Town planners usually come from places many miles away from the places that they have come to redevelop. They take the city and turn it into a wasteland where wind howls down concrete tunnels, graffiti from aerosol cans is the only feature that breaks the monotony, and the same neon signs proclaim the same neon legends in every city in the land from Milton Keynes to Glasgow, from Bradford to Liverpool.

The multinationals and the developers have moved in. More has meant less choice; bigger has meant all the same. And people hurry away from the cities because no one lives in them any more and at night, after the thrill-seekers have gone from disco and club, the cities are the dead haunts of the bag people and the villains. And for doing all this the planners win awards.

CRABS AND LOBSTERS _____

Pour whisky and sand on the affected parts; the crabs and lobsters will then get drunk and stone each other to death.

CRIME _____

It all started with pencils from Woolworth's RONALD BIGGS

Since you brought the fiddles, why don't you guys give us a toon or two? CHICAGO, ST VALENTINE'S DAY

I'm innocent! POPE GUILTY

Crime pays BARABAS

In the olden days in England, you could be hung for stealing a sheep or a loaf of bread. However, if a sheep stole a loaf of bread and gave it to you, you would only be tried for receiving, a crime punishable by forty lashes with the cat or the dog, whichever was handy. If you stole a dog and were caught, you were punished with twelve rabbit punches although it was hard to find rabbits big enough or strong enough to punch you. So they usually burned you through the gristle of the nose instead.

For any crimes more serious than these, compulsory public nail biting was the usual punishment. This was considered a terrible punishment and if you'd seen the state of people's nails in those days then you'd understand why. Whole towns would queue up to get their nails bitten by criminals in the stocks since nail clippers had not been invented and it was the only way of getting a manicure.

Nowadays criminals are locked up in prison for a long time with no one to talk to and nothing to do which is rather like curing somebody of pneumonia by throwing them in a freezing cold lake.

If you fancy being a criminal then you have to start young by stealing things from other babies in the next pram or forging your own birth certificate. But to be honest, crime isn't a lot of fun and if you're looking for excitement you're better off sticking to things such as ludo or snakes and ladders or strip darts.

CRITICS _____

And lo on the eighth day Eric did take up a piece of animal dung and breathe on it and it did become a creature that did walk into bars and fall down and Eric called it a 'Critic'
THE BOOK OF ERIC CH III V6

Those who can do, those who can't write about it
ALBERT BERNARD SHAW

It doesn't matter what you do – write, fly pigeons, clear tables in a café, swallow swords, paint, carve budgie bungs, sing, juggle with loaded mousetraps – there will always be somebody prepared to make a living out of telling you how you're doing it wrong, or not quite right. The shortest piece of criticism was a piece in the *Cleck-heaton Albion* reviewing a play *Good Time* by a local dramatist Ernest Plank. The headline above the review read GOOD TIME AT THE BIJOU and underneath was the review: 'It wasn't.'

'Nobody is above criticism' is a saying probably coined by critics in a moment of enlightened self-interest and isn't in fact true, because if it was then critics would have critics and they in their turn would have critics too. The result would be books such as *A Critical Appraisal of the Critical Writings of the Critics of Shakespeare's Critics*.

Let's face it, most people know whether they've enjoyed a play or a film or a book and don't really need a critic

to form their opinions for them. Standards in the arts are not raised by critics but by the artists themselves. If we have to have critics then let's save newsprint and just have reviews such as

Lady Windermere's Fan Apollo, Solihull
4/10 Must try harder
or
Audience 6
Actors 0

How long will it be before people watching men digging holes in the road will produce cards reading 5.6, 5.6, 5.9, 5.3, like ice-skating judges and go away muttering, 'Nowhere near as good as Mick Doonan's gang putting the new drains in the abbatoir at Gland Street' and, 'You should have seen the Clancy gang laying the foundations for the law courts in 1957, some of their pick work was pure poetry etc. etc. etc.'?

CRUELFINGER, CHARLES

In 1881 Charles Cruelfinger of Yeovil kept 17 live budgerigars in his underpants because, he said, their flapping kept his 'Antipodes in a state of flux' or, as somebody more crudely put it, 'They kept the wind whistlin' round his cobblers on hot days'. He was transported to Van Diemen's Land in 1883 for having 'unnatural relations with a post-box on the Queen's highway'.

In Australia he became a bushranger, joining Mad Jack McGurk's band of outlaws but died when he tried to hold up a night-train single handed without a lamp. The driver of the train said they didn't realize they'd been held up

until they reached their destination and found a cocked pistol stuck in the front of the train and the marks of a head on the smoke box cover. A passenger thought he heard someone shout, 'Stop! This is a stick –' but paid no attention to it because he'd been drinking and often heard things after 14 jugs of Knockin' Nellie's Nightmare Juice.

DANCING

A form of eroticism not to be confused with sex in any way. It consists largely in moving about rhythmically with somebody of the opposite sex without inserting anything anywhere at any time.

Dancing cannot result directly in pregnancy or disease except splintered feet and coronaries.

At one time dancing was a way of disguising the fact that people were in fact copulating standing up and most dancing was done with couples clinched together jumping up and down around a maypole with a couple of shawm and crumhorn players and someone banging a tambour to keep the rhythm going.

It was the Puritans who put an end to this practice as well as discontinuing the tradition of kings wearing heads on their shoulders. The Puritans introduced long distance dancing in order 'to dissuade the rude peasauntrie from leepinge, dauncinge and couplinge in a lewde, lascivious and papist waye'. Long-distance dancing totally ruled out any possibility of cheekiness since, by law, people could only dance with partners who were at least 60 miles away. People in Bury St Edmunds, for example, used to dance only with people in Hartlepool until the Restoration.

The definition of dancing as the ritual extension of man's attempt to explain his own relationship with God and Nature can be discounted on the grounds that most priests and gardeners are lousy dancers.

Dancing in the twentieth century falls into three categories –

Ballet or art dancing If you can prance about in a leotard with a batting box on and jump up in the air with whopping big ballerinas on your head then fair play to you.

Art dancing can be very strange and can involve things like impersonating bricks and stone walls. I did a bit of this once as part of a course I was doing. While I was dancing 'A Day in the Life of a Furry Caterpillar' a girl student, who was dancing 'Two and a Half Hours in the Life of A Thrush', nearly pecked me to death and tore a ligament trying to fly up to her nest with me.

Ballroom dancing   For this you need yards and yards of tulle, several gallons of hair oil and years of training in jungle warfare.

Disco dancing   This is the best form of contraceptive ever invented since the music is so loud you can't chat anyone up. Everybody dances apart without touching anyone else, so presumably they all go home alone and kick the cat.

If you want to get out of all the noise and sweaty jumping about with no prospect of any post-coital glow at the end of it then tell them you've got a bone in your leg.

DENTISTS _____

Nobody likes going to the dentist. Dentists don't even like going to the dentist. The main reason, of course, is that they hurt. But unless you want to walk round with teeth like a mouthful of cigarette ends and breath like the inside of a guerilla's combat boot, you'll have to go to them.

Silly Dentist Joke

'This little prick won't hurt.'
'Oh yes you will – you did last time.'

The best way to avoid having a dentist hurt you too much
is to take a small revolver with you.

DINING OUT _____

*Throw a stick across the table, if the sausages chase it go
somewhere else* 'The Egon Ronay Guide to Transport
Cafés'

Don't speak with someone in your mouth MRS CANNIBAL

Dining out is OK if you have got the money and if you like
eating foreign food because apart from Harry Ramsdens',
Old Bagdale Hall, Whitby, and a few oyster bars and
north country restaurants there aren't many places I can
think of that serve traditional English fare, unless you
fancy putting on your tuxedo and grabbing your bird with
her stole and orchid and getting her a stringy meat,
collapsed sprout and grey potato dinner (jam roly-poly,
tea, bread'n'butter thrown in and a merry christmas to our
patrons) at Gear Box Harry's on the Great North Road.

When dining out in posh nosh gaffs, expect to pay more
for the meal than you would for a small bungalow in
Chingford. Remember, too, that the waiter will think
you're a right pratt. If you've got more money than him
he'll resent you for it; if you've got less money than him
he'll despise you for it.

In an Indian restaurant expect that, after pub closing time, strange men will fall through the door wild eyed and listless, call the waiter 'Sabu' and fall asleep with their heads in bowls of chicken madras off the bone. Such drunks also manage to have a fine time with papadums which explode in their hands into a shower of lethal fragments. After the Great Bombay Duck Disaster in Birmingham in 1978, 15 people were taken to hospital with severe papadum lacerations.

Indian restaurants also manage to serve the hottest cups of coffee anywhere in the world. The technique is simple. First they boil the water and milk with superheated steam until only a Venusian could live in it. They next heat the cup and saucer with a blowlamp so that, when you finally get it all on the table, you need a furnace workers' mittens to pick it up.

A word on curries. Real Indian food has a much wider variety than you might come to expect if you only use your local 'Eleventeen pints I'm bloody starvin' – I could go a curry' Taj Mahal-type emporium. Such restaurants have red wallpaper, a picture of the Taj Mahal and low lighting so that you can't see the stains on the carpet. They serve only three types of curries:

1 the 'that wasn't as bad as I expected' curry
2 the 'it sneaks up on you from behind, this one' curry, and
3 the 'I'd better tell the missus to put some toilet paper in the fridge' curry.

As an old-time rock-band-musician curry-addict I'll leave you with this warning: never go to a curry house near a down-town pub unless you like fighting, throwing up and sitting on the can for four hours a day. Always aim up-town. It's more expensive but you'll save on bog paper.

DO-IT-YOURSELF_____

It cuts out the middle man and you don't have to get dressed up ONAN

I must have got the plans upside down ICARUS

I've seen some lovely buffalo-patterned wallpaper in the shops CAVEWOMAN

Since time immoral man has been forced to do little jobs at weekends. Emerging from the mud he was probably asked to put a few extra stones in the hovel so his mate could keep her nick-nacks out of the primordial slime. With ochre and stick he made cack-handed attempts at interior wall painting with the mammoths of Altamira breathing down his neck. Shakespeare would have written at least another 400 plays if it wasn't for Anne Hathaway moaning at him all the time to get up on the roof and thatch the cottage. How much better to have had those wonderful plays finished: *Son of Hamlet, Macbeth Rides Again, King Lear Meets Godzilla*.

Do-it-Yourself was invented by Onan. You can always tell a DIY fanatic as you walk through his garden gates – the electric eye closes them on you. He waves a bandaged hand at you through the window. You put your hand on the front door and find that it's just been painted – he wasn't waving, he was telling you to go round the back. Once inside you lose things down joins in the furniture, his wife is usually a nervous wreck because everything in the house either falls on her, traps her or gives her an electric shock. One weekend when he brings his electric drill out she's going to throw a bucket of water over him.

And have you noticed how bad things usually are when they've been done themselves? That's an attractive piece of furniture you say. Knocked it together myself he says – only took me a couple of weekends. Got the plans out of *Practical Crisismaker*. And just as you are going to ask him what it does he leans on it and it falls over broken and spewing out all the things nobody wants but won't throw away.

At one time, the DIY craze was flushing doors and millions of craftsmen-made panelled doors vanished under 6′ × 2½′ shrouds of hardboard on countless surburban Sunday afternoons. The kids were kept busy handing the panel pins to Dad who kept proudly hitting himself with the hammer until his thumb and first two fingers looked like a pound of badly wrapped salami. He screamed at the children who cried and wanted to go out to play. He kept them there because he wanted them to see how he, the great hunter, also kept the cave a nice place to live in. Thus in countless surburban rooms from Altamira to New Jersey has man destroyed his children's love for him and his own ability to pick up anything smaller than a sauce bottle.

They tell you it's cheaper to DIY. It is *never* cheaper by the time you've bought all the tools and materials at the DIY store's prices, broken fingers, got divorced, put nails through the pipes and flooded the house, and put nails through the mains cable so that everyone who touches the new coat rack you've put up in the hall ends up on their backs staring at the ceiling of the spare room.

The cost of getting the experts in to mend everything after is too much. Pay them in the first place.

The worst example of DIY was the boy who stuck his finger in the dyke's hole in Holland. It was all right as an emergency measure but it started off a rash of human plug-using that was only stopped in this century.

If called upon to DIY

1 throw a fit and froth at the mouth and claim that you are allergic to heights, putty, paint, nails and anything sharp or heavy;
2 saw the rungs off the ladders;
3 paint the glass in the windows and paper over the door;
4 claim that you're putting at least 11 men out of work, dwell on their starving families, children crying for bread, etc.;
5 picket the tool box;
6 sniff all tubes of glue, tins of paint, etc., click fingers and say, 'Far out, too much man, what a trip wowee etc.' She'll either throw them away or leave you at it in which case you'll probably end up meaning what you say;
7 if all else fails, burn the house down.

DOCTORS

Doctors bury their mistakes WINSTON CHURCHILL
Churchill buried his mistakes DOCTOR
The only good doctor is a dead one MRS CRIPPEN

You can catch more things in doctor's waiting rooms than you go in with. People sit there coughing germs and breathing all sorts of diseases into the air. The best way to avoid this is to go in coughing more than they are, whooping and sniffing and spluttering until they either all clear out or offer to let you go in first.

The first doctor was a Greek called Hippocrates. He had not always been a doctor. His first job was making large boxes for big wild animals. He became a doctor by chance when Agamemnon punched him on the nose and made it bleed. Hippocrates (waterhorse box) cured the nose bleed by putting a back door down the back of his shirt. He was surprised by this, particularly since he had only done it to gain attention. People saw this and came to Hippocrates for advice which at first largely consisted in telling people to put doors down their necks. Eventually he discovered that it was only the keys that really helped so from then on he just made people put keys down their necks for everything. As a result of this a lot of people died. Most people at that time were locked out, too.

Doctors are all right but remember they too get ill, particularly as they spend so much time with sick people. He's bound to catch something and might even give it you if you ask him nicely.

Silly Doctor Joke

'Doctor, doctor, I kept thinking I'm Donald Duck.'
'Don't worry you're just quacking up.'

DOGS _____

Here doggy, here doggy . . . oh shit! LORD BASKERVILLE
Out damned Spot LADY MACBETH

It is a known fact that dog-owners get to look like their pets and vice versa. Marilyn Monroe's borzoi was pro-

posed to by three Arabian princes and a soya-bean mil-
lionaire from Macgillycuddy's Reeks, Eire, while Sophia
Loren's poodle and Britt Ekland's chihuahua have been
followed home on more than one occasion. On the other
hand, Margaret Thatcher's bull terrier has been known to
make strong men cringe and small children go into uncon-
trollable gibbering fits.

How to train a dog

1 tell it what to do
2 if it doesn't do it, kick it
3 if it doesn't do it again, kick it again
4 if it still doesn't do it get another dog

Dogs are not much good at complicated things like washing cars or putting plugs on electric cables but they can be trained to fetch a paper or at the very least not to crap in the house, or, if mixed up in training, to fetch the paper and then crap on it. If you do send your dog to get the paper make sure it knows which one to get and don't give it too much money or it might not come back.

DRINK

I drink therefore I am   DESCARTES, French polisher

Drink is not the same thing as drunk, as Chomsky once said – although he was, in fact, armpits to breakfast at the time. Drink can be a relaxing influence, a promoter of well-being, a calming medication, a socially acceptable drug which has killed far more people than cannabis.

Drunks, however, can be a pain in the sitons (*see* **Drunks**).

DRUNKS

There is some hidden cosmic force akin to magnetism, telepathy, ESP, astrology or dowsing that propels drunks towards those people who want to have least to do with them and keeps them in orbit round them while they bore them witless, gibbering incomprehensibilities and spraying them with spit, potato crisp flecks and dentures. Occasionally the law of alcoholic attraction 'like forces repel' finds exceptions and drunks can be found talking to each other; the result can be incredible and usually bears as much resemblance to communication as canaries do to cheese.

If a drunk buttonholes you, you have a few alternatives

1 act as though you've been hijacked and wave for help
2 fall on the floor frothing at the mouth (recommended)
3 try and act more drunk than he/she is and he'll move away in fear.

EARLY CHRISTIANS_____

Before the days of Kitty-Kat and Catecombs, lions were fed on a diet of early Christians. This was a bit rough on most early Christians although those who arrived late usually only lost a leg or a finger or so. The early Christians, steeled in their faith by persecution, decided to spread the word of the Lord all over the World.

This has resulted in almost 2,000 years of wars, pogroms, witch-hunts and inquisitions and has left us with the situation in Northern Ireland today. Some people think it's a shame that the lions didn't have better appetites.

ECONOMICS_____

Economics is the study of the value and meaning of J. K. Galbraith.

Economics, as every schoolboy knows, is the science concerned with how some people make money by working hard, some people make a lot more money by telling the rest of the people to work hard and some people do nothing at all and get paid very well for it. It is also the study of how, like government, nobody has ever been able to get it right and how at bottom, the Common People have always been the ones who've been caught in the khazi with the door locked from the outside. How useless economics is in everyday life can be seen from the fact that there aren't many rich economists apart from those who write books or advise governments on how to cock it up.

Economics is also concerned with such topics as value. For instance, a glass of water is worth more to a bedouin in the Sahara than it would be if he was in the Finchley High Street. Mind you, if he was in the Finchley High Street, his camel might get knocked down. If he was in Golders Green, he would get knocked down.

Another topic of concern to economists is free enterprise and the profit motive, i.e. greed. The ultimate examples of free enterprise are the sawn-off shotgun and the nylon stocking. I agree with Proudhon that all property is theft, but I'm afraid I don't know what to do about it. Control of the means of production basically asks the question, 'Which came first the chicken or the egg or the investment in the chicken hut, or the wood and nails? And does it really matter if you can't afford a frying pan anyway?'

ELVES, GOBLINS, FAIRIES, GNOMES, POOKAS AND TROLLS

If you suffer from any or all of these things either

1 Stop eating the funny-coloured mushrooms
2 Stop sleeping in the woods on midsummer nights

3 Offer to be their agent and get them a job in a circus
4 Alternatively, shave the affected parts and paint over
   with a solution of potassium permanganate and bitter
   aloes.

EXECUTIVES _____

*An executive is someone who dresses smart because he isn't and
who moves fast because he doesn't want to be found out*
ERIC GRIBLEY QC.

I don't want to say much about executives other than what
can be worse than the sight of these clean-cut young
company men pushing each other, brown-nosed, up the
company ladder clutching their pink *Financial Times* and
their daggers; playing golf with the right people; marrying
the right girls; joining the right clubs; working their way
to a company paunch, a company ulcer and a company
coronary – sublime in the knowledge that their clogged
arteries have been won on the back of some poor unfortunate who lives far away from the redbrick executive estate
where our hypertense friend full of gateaux, coq au vin,
mortgages and school bills has his last coronary while
hitching his powerboat to the back of his Triumph Dolo-
mite.

FAILURE _____

If at first you don't succeed pull the legs off the spider
ROBERT THE BRUTAL

A decent honourable catastrophic failure is better than a middling success – any day. So if you're going to fail, do it properly.

FILM STARS_____

At one time everybody wanted to be a film star but there weren't enough names to go round. Here are a few names that could help the budding Rock Hudson or Tab Hunter on his way to Hollywood.

Troy Weight
Rock Bottom
Kurt Answers
Julie Arranged
Yul B. Sori
Hank R. Chief
Grace B. Formeals
Dustin Case
Sonny Disposition
Jock Und
Carmel Knowledge
Spencer Vere Innit
Rip Tights

FOOD

I'll just try another surfeit of them lampreys   KING JOHN

After 2,000 years of civilization, Man has succeeded in producing the perfect way to destroy food – motorway cafés and BR food.

Food is a dangerous article – too much food makes you fat, too little food makes you dead.

FOOD: FADS AND ISMS

Vegetarianism, based on the principle that vegetables have no feelings, was a popular food 'ism' until the discovery of vegetable communications by Professor Ström in 1979. Working with radishes, Professor Ström was able to decipher more than 3,000 separate radish utterances which later formed the basis of his *The Roots of Radish: Radix Radix*, a linguistic transcription of a polemic conversation on the Quantum Theory and whether Queen Victoria had a beard, between the Professor and four of the most intelligent radishes. This was to revolutionize man's view of his own relationship with the vegetable kingdom. The first effects of this discovery was a rise in the number of free-range leek farms and potato ranches, while carrot herding became a stable feature of chalk upland rural communities.

People sickened at the slaughter of cabbages, sprouts, beets etc. became Atmospharian living on fresh air, water, old ironing boards and synthetic blotting paper, until their leader, Veronica Bag, was found to be a ventriloquist manipulating the cabbages. This discovery discredited the movement.

FORMS

Most people hate filling in forms – not only are they time wasting they are often confusing and at times insulting and intrusive. Why, when buying a food mixer, do you have to fill in a form stating your age, address, height and marital status? The best way to screw the system is to fill the form in correctly – the computer will explode.

FUNERALS

Rules for the game of 'Funeral'

A game of chance for two or more players.

1 One or more of the players must be dead
2 Some of the other players must be not dead
3 The object of the game is for the not-dead players (called mourners) to get rid of the dead players (called the deceased)
4 During the game everyone dresses in black except the dead players who can wear what they like

The game of Funerals has many variations, commonest played are Hot Funerals and Cold Funerals. (Burial at Sea does not count as it is a water sport, like sex in the bath.) Hot Funeral is becoming very popular, particularly in the South of England; in the North of England Cold Funeral is still the most prevalent form of the game . . .

Cold Funeral

1 The dead player gets in long box – 'the wooden over-coat' or 'plywood suit' as it is sometimes known

THE
UNKNOWN
MOURNER

2 The not-dead players drive him slowly round holding up all the traffic
3 The dead player is then hidden in the ground
4 The rest of the players then eat ham and drink tea in a cold, unfriendly pub room

Hot Funerals

As in the game of cold funerals but after driving round slowly the dead player is hidden in a very hot fire before the other players go on to the ham etc.

Irish Funerals

A variant of Hot and Cold Funerals that should never be attempted by those of a weak or nervous disposition. The dead player stays in the house propped up in the corner smiling and all the other players take turns at singing, crying, drinking, fighting, falling down and immorality. Then the dead player (if he has not been lost or taken home by some not-dead player by mistake) is hidden in the ground and for years afterwards everybody tries to re-member where he is hidden. This ending to the game is called A Stalemate or, depending upon how long it takes, A Very Stalemate.

Variants on the basic game

These can be introduced to make Basic Funerals more interesting.

1 The Mourner Nobody Knows. This is a guessing game and can provide hours of endless fun. Some typical guesses might be:
   a) it was his/her fancy man/woman
   b) it's a plainclothes policeman. They're suspicious about the way he died
   c) he's a talent scout from Rent a Mourner
   d) he's from the Egon Ronay Good Funeral Tea Guide

2 Dropping the Coffin. This is a good variant, especially good for a laugh at Irish Funerals. Mourners should shout things like 'That'll wake the bugger up', 'He was always fond of a drop', 'Nice of you to drop in, Arthur', 'What a let down', etc. etc.

3 Shouting out generally is recommended to liven the game up especially Hot Funerals which tend to be over too quick unless something is done to break them up a bit. For instance, 'Frying tonight', 'That reminds me I left the chip pan on the stove', 'She always did moan about being cold', 'Did you pay the gas bill?', 'That's a waste of a good suit', 'How do you like it Bert, medium, well done or rare?', 'He always said he'd go out in a blaze', etc.

4 Reading the Will. This can sometimes be the best part of the game and can, if it's a good one, result in arguments, fights and sometimes more dead players, in which case the game starts all over again.

GARAGES

Garages work on the principle that God made three things: cars, time and money. And God's first commandment unto Moses the Mechanic was: 'And thou shalt say it's not the parts, it's the labour.'

The Armchair Anarchist knows that there is nothing he can do to beat the garage system. If you take your brand new car in for its first service they'll let a spotty little Herbert who's just left school climb all over it, drip brake fluid on the paintwork, and adjust the tappits so the radio's giving out exhaust fumes and you've got Terry Wogan coming out of the heater. He'll drop a spanner in somewhere important and you won't know anything about it until chewed up pieces of vanadium steel start firing out of the exhaust breaking windows and hitting stray dogs, then in the middle of the M6 the car will grind to a halt and you'll discover a girlie magazine, a half-eaten pork pie, a packet of curry-flavoured crisps and a brew can left under the bonnet. If you complain they'll either say, 'We've never had anything like this before' or, 'You know what you did wrong of course, you've been driving it'.

When you first take your car into the garage they'll lift up the bonnet, Fred will call Jim over and say, ''ave a look at this Jim.' And Jim will say, 'I 'aven't seen one of them for years.'

'But it's only 12 months old,' you say.

'Well they've stopped making them now,' says Fred. 'You can't get the parts any more. It's a pity they stopped makin' them they used to be good cars, old Jim 'ere worked on 'em all the time didn't you Jim? There's a bloke down the road breaking one up for scrap – we might be able to get a few bits from him for it, but it'll cost a few bob to put right. 'Course they made cars in them days, 12 months ago, it's a dying art now, you couldn't get lads today to work like we used to etc. etc. etc.'

The best thing you can do is either buy a new one or just arrange to have all your money paid straight into the garage every week and collect what's left on a Friday night.

GOD _____

If there is a God let him strike me dead with lightning – you see! nothing hap—aargh!

Now this is a big one. God did not just appear and make the world. Things don't happen like that! God's been around for a long time and got the job because he knew somebody who recommended him.

102

God has many disguises: mostly he goes around in a long white nightie and beard but when danger threatens he nips into a phone box, puts his underpants on outside his trousers and comes out as the Paraclete or Holy Ghost. As such he can fly, break through walls and wiggle his ears. God III or God Jun. is another of God's disguises and can walk on water, cure the lame and make cupboards. All in all, they make a good team. Exists in other religions as Jahweh, Jehovah, Zeus Buddha and Eric (*see* **Bible**).

GOLD

A soft malleable metal relatively scarce in distribution. It is mined deep in the earth by poor men who then give it to rich men who immediately bury it back in the earth in great prisons although gold hasn't done anything to them.

GOODBYES AND FAREWELLS

Goodbyes and farewells are usually lengthy and distressing and are best avoided. If you've got to go then go quickly, without a long lingering kiss because it lets the cold air into the hall and her old man will come out moaning about the cost of his central heating.

'Get thee to a nunnery' is about as neat a bit of goodbyeing I've heard in a long time but the best bum's rush in

Shakespeare is without doubt Lady Macbeth's 'Stand not upon the order of your going but go!' It's a wonder she didn't set damned Spot on them.

As far as farewells are concerned, one of the best is Captain Oates's 'I'm going for a walk' as he went out into a

blizzard near the South Pole. A walk where? To the pub? Round the corner for a quick one? No, Scott and the lads knew where he was going so they never bothered asking. Which is a bit of a shame really because it means that now we'll never know where he went.

One of the most famous farewells is probably Nelson's to Hardy and is depicted best of all in Eric Scroat's play *With Hardy at Nelson's End*. The characters are Hardy, Nelson and two Irishmen.

Nelson [mortally wounded]   Kismet, Hardy, Kismet.

1st Irishman   I knew that Nelson was a turd burglar.

2nd Irishman   He didn't say kiss me, he said kismet.

1st Irishman   Is that a brand name?

2nd Irishman   No, he means it's his fate.

1st Irishman   I'll take his shoes off for him then.

2nd Irishman   Look at him, shot in his prime.

1st Irishman   I thought it was his eye.

2nd Irishman   That was last time.

1st Irishman   Where did they get him this time?

2nd Irishman   In the cockpit.

1st Irishman   In that case there's no hope for him.

GOURMETS

Gourmets are little rubber rings to stop ropes, wires, cables, etc. fraying when they go through holes in metal, wood etc.

GOVERNMENT _____

A government official is anyone who can scrape up 51% of the votes cast by the 40% of the voters who could be bothered to vote out of the 60% of the eligible population. Thus democracy ensures that something like 13% of the population choose the government.

If a country gets the government it deserves then we in Britain must have done something terribly wrong at some time.

In Britain, government is effectively in the hands not of the politicians but of the high-ranking civil servants who run the various ministries since they have access to all the information and ultimately have to transfer the power. Thus real power is in the hands of a class of people drawn in the main from Oxbridge and centred in London around the main ministries. When you consider their links with the army, the police and the aristocracy it's not much wonder that little has changed in the last 80 years.

GREAT BALD SWAMP HEDGEHOG___

The Great Bald Swamp Hedgehog of Billericay displays, in courtship, his single prickle and does impressions of Holiday Inn desk clerks. Since this means him standing motionless for enormous periods of time he is often eaten in full display by the Great Bald Swamp Hedgehog Eater.

GREEK MYTHOLOGY (A brief guide)

DILDO   The goddess of cornucopia players and saxophonists.

DUMBO   The god with special responsibility for party conversation and manhole covers.

TERMINUS   The god of tram drivers.

DOMINO   The god of those who suffer from measles.

GRIMSHAWE, ERIC

This anarchist was responsible for designing the International Clowns' Centre in Dundee, a building with sprinklers in the floor, no windows and doors that fell off every time somebody opened them. The building was designed in the shape of a huge pair of baggy pants topped off by a gigantic red nose and blew down in the tremendous gales of the winter of 1967 while a clown convention was being held in the giant custard pie at the heart of the building, 37 clowns being cooked to death. It is thought that they could have been saved had not other clowns repeatedly tripped the firemen, sprayed them with their own hoses and told them to look up in the sky while they then poured buckets of whitewash down the fronts of their trousers.

    Grimshawe also designed an aquaduct to carry the ferry across the Humber, a greenhouse with brick windows, an underground tower for people with vertigo and a building shaped like a dead chicken for the egg marketing board.

It was only after he had destroyed the centres of most of the cities and towns in Britain, had designed and built several motorways, concreted Dartmoor to turn it into London's eighth airport and had built a swimming-pool where the balconies were filled with water and the spectators sat in a dry, tiled, sunken enclosure that it was realized

1 that he was totally mad
2 that he had influenced Le Corbusier and almost every other architect that had followed
3 he had made a lot of money.

GROMETS

Gromets are people who really enjoy their food, e.g. Clement Freud and Fatty Arbuckle.

HALIFAX _____

The people of Halifax invented the trampoline. During the Victorian period the tripe-dressers of Halifax stretched tripe across a large wooden frame and jumped up and down on it to 'tender and dress' it. The tripoline, as they called it, degenerated into becoming the apparatus for a spectator sport.

The people of Halifax also invented the hamonium, a device for castrating pigs during Sunday service.

HATS
Mainly for men _____

If you're going to wear a hat, you've got to accept the fact that men who can wear hats and look good are about as commonplace as frostbite in the Sahara.

If you're going to wear a hat do it properly, go right over the top – wear one that looks like a piece of symbiotic fungus, get one that will make strange men follow you home and old ladies bless themselves as you pass. Don't try and hide the fact that it's a hat, don't skulk about as though you've got nothing on your head and look surprised when someone points it out saying, 'Oh that! I've never noticed it before. I wonder how long that's been there etc. etc.'

If you're going to wear a hat you've got to have style. I saw a bloke recently who was the image of Che Guevera,

slim, dark, confidently handsome, muscular, bearded, a keen-eyed revolutionary in denims and combat jacket reading Marx, propped up against a bookshelf in my local library. He even had a beret on. It was this that let him down. It was stuck on his head like the crust on a pie, straight on and puffed up, a green felt meringue rising off his head. If he'd tried to lead a revolution like that, he'd have been laughed out of the jungle.

HOUSES

This is one helluva basement   DANTE

I'll huff and I'll puff   BIG BAD WOLF DEMOLITION COMPANY

Not windows again, we had windows last night
HANSEL AND GRETEL

Most people live in houses in Britain. 'A roof over your head', 'A home of your own', 'An Englishman's home is his castle' are words bandied about by building societies as though bandy words were going out of fashion. They talk about owning your own home as though it was a big deal. They don't ever point out that, since you can't take anything much beyond the cemetery gates apart from what you lie down in, you can't 'own' anything much in this world. Having not pointed this out, they then go on not to point out that the money they lend you with interest will take you the rest of your life to pay off, leaving something for your family to row over.

The language estate agents use makes Quasimodo look straight.

'Desirable' – then why are they selling it?

'Compact' – the mice are hunchbacked.

'Recently decorated' – they've slapped a coat of cheap paint everywhere.

'Recently modernized' – they've stuck hardboard sheets over all the panelled doors and chopped all the mouldings off.

'Period' – it's got dry rot and rising damp.

'Interesting' – you have to bend to see out of the windows.

'Needs some renovation' – the woodworm holding hands is the only thing keeping it standing.

Until the first Anarchist Prime Minister gets elected, there isn't a lot you can do.

INSANITY

We don't know what came over me   JEKYLL AND HYDE
Depressed? Me? Ha ha ha ha ha ha BANG
DEAD MANIC DEPRESSIVE

Vincent Van Gogh
Cut a bit off
When they asked him why
He replied 'Yer What, Pardon? Whad did you say? etc.'

If all the world thought they were Napoleon or Shakespeare and you thought you weren't, you would be locked up as a nutter; yet the society that would put you away today for thinking you were a daffodil has invented germ warfare, the bomb, insurance, assembly lines, the TV dinner, high-rise flats, bingo and instant mashed potato.

They said Guy Fawkes was mad because he wanted to blow up Parliament; if that's true then in Britain today something like fifty million people must be mad.

KINGS

Today, Alphonse, I shall dress in your dustbinman's clothes and go out and see the world while you shall dress in my royal robes and stay in the palace EX-KING FRED THE MAD, dustbinman of Pishtenstein.

Go back! Go back! Goblackle! Gobbleablkel! Gobbleooble bleble! KING CANUTE

Kings are strange things. At one time, touching the hem of a king's robe was thought to cure the toucher of most diseases, especially leprosy and the pox. But you couldn't get it on prescription.

The first king was in fact no more than a robber chief who became strong enough to subdue all the other chieftains and the peoples under their command. He used this as an excuse for levying taxes and living in the best hut in the area, a practice which has continued to this day, the only difference being that in those days the kings did at least lead their men into battle and stood a fair chance of being killed. Kings today are of real use only in fairy stories.

LAVATORY SEATS_____

Things you can't catch off lavatory seats

> dandruff
> toothache
> bankruptcy
> fallen arches
> hangovers
> ingrowing toenails

Things you can catch off lavatory seats

> broken legs
> termites
> splinters
> dry rot and deathwatch beetle especially in wooden legs
> zenophobia (if there's no door)
> *nonequuspeditis* (one leg longer than the other) often found
> in people who have no lock on the toilet door.

LOVE _____

*If you were the only girl in the world you'd have to have a
strong back*   OLD FOLK SONG

*If it wasn't for love all the songwriters would be digging holes
and emptying trashcans*   JOHN DONNE

Love must be one of the most painful afflictions known to
Man and is as curable as a bite from a rattlesnake. To be in

love is to suffer the torments of the damned: to wait with beating heart and sweaty palms, a lump in the throat and a tilt in the kilt until the object of love arrives, to fall on his or her every word and to believe that the universe would stop if he or she were not there.

Not only are you a pain to yourself when in love, you are also a severe pain in the Tierra Del Feugo to everybody else. Lovesick human beings are about as much fun to be with as a train smash. You can get more intelligent conversation from a bowl of cornflakes.

Love rhymes with 'moon', 'spoon', 'June', 'mortgage' and 'dirty nappies'; it also produces hot flushes, overtipping and can lead to fights in pubs, e.g. 'I'm the only one allowed to call my wife a flyblown piece of elephant poop'.

If you want to keep yourself to yourself (Onan did) and lead a fairly uncomplicated life without appearing in the *News of the World* – then don't fall in love. Love is costly, time consuming and when taken in excess can lead to hiccups, temporary loss of speech, rough skin on elbows and knees, melancholia, lack of concentration, loss of weight, permanent fixed grins and carelessness with hot objects.

LOVE CUSTOMS AROUND THE WORLD

When the Ngdanga tribe of West Africa hold their moon love ceremonies the men of the tribe bang their heads on sacred trees until they get a nose bleed which usually cures them of that.

When young men of the Strirtsxi tribe of New Guinea want to show their love for a maiden they leave gifts at her hut door such as four or five of her enemies' heads, a television video game or a couple of electric eels. Only the bravest of warriors can catch the electric eels since, to catch one, the warrior has to swim underwater with a roll of fuse wire and a pair of pliers in his hand and a light bulb in his mouth until the bulb goes 'Fuding' when he has to grab the eel and sling it on the shore with a pair of rubber gloves.

Fierce competition can result in a pretty girl with the requisite number of umbrella spines through her lips, being inundated with heads and eels. Hence the saying 'Head over eels in love'.

MACCLESFIELD _____

People from Macclesfield are fed up with being laughed at because of their habit of tucking their vests into their socks.

MARRIAGE _____

Take my wife – I wish you would   'RED NOSE COMIX'

My wife doesn't understand me   DEAF MUTE SERBOCROAT MORMON MARRIED TO PERUVIAN ATHEIST INSOMNIAC WOODCARVER.

Not tonight darling, I've got a headache   ANN BOLEYN
We'll soon fix that   HENRY VIII

I saw what you wrote about me in them epistles and I'm going to take the kids and go back to me mother's in Tarsus
MRS ST PAUL

My old grandad always said that getting married is like fancying cream cake and then having to eat it for the rest of your life. I couldn't put it better myself.

MECHANICAL THINGS _____

Most Armchair Anarchists know that mechanical things are made, in the main, so that they will go wrong. Try not to go near them or pretend that you don't care if they do break down; in some cases you should actually show contempt for the objects, particularly electrical gadgets such as vacuum cleaners and lawnmowers and shout things such as, 'What a stupid lawnmower you are' and, 'There's nothing clever about being a machine for sucking up muck'. It won't stop them breaking down but you may feel a bit better.

It's not always the big things that break down either; neither, for that matter, are the big things necessarily important. If your car breaks down you can walk, if a tin opener breaks down you might starve. Most mechanical things function according to Job's Law.

1 If it is within the function of a thing to work it is also within its function not to work.
2 Anything that has not been working will probably start working when you take it back to the shop and will stop again when you get home.
3 Things with moveable bits will trap your fingers.
4 If you try to mend anything you will break it beyond repair.

The last of Job's Laws states that if there are any boils knocking about, I'll get them; while Boyle's Law states that if there are any jobs knocking about, I won't even get an interview.

124

MONETARISM

This is the theory that the supply of money must be controlled no matter who gets hurt and that ultimately only those firms/organizations/people fit to survive will survive. This is basically the philosophy of the jungle and was followed by Tsar Nicholas, Louis XV and the Emperor of China until the starving mobs kicked in their Palace gates.

Monetarists usually condemn spending money on anything other than the army, the police force or bomb shelters.

MONEY

The only thing money can't buy is abject poverty   ANON

Many a mickle makes a muckle   ALLY, BRUCE, TAM, IAN, JOCK, ANGUS, WULLY AND MORAG MICKLE, MUCKLE-MAKERS.

Armchair Anarchists know that the possession of money is a totally artificial substitute for the true coinage of life: sunsets, the sound of children laughing, the smell of a pine forest, the feel of a good book, the taste of a fine wine, a night in good company, the kiss of the sun on your face, the sound of surf on a moonlit cove . . . but since no one's going to thank you for putting two tickets to Morecambe in their pay packets instead of seventy-five quid it looks as though we're stuck with what Chaucer called 'The boyle on the erse of the Werlde'.

How did money enter into our lives?

Before money was invented Man grew or caught or dug up all that he needed – roots, nuts, berries, wild pigs and fish were all about him and his for the gathering. Then somebody invented television video games and men who had no way of getting them any other way were forced to barter for them.

Barter worked like this. First you killed some beast to eat but, since you would probably only eat three legs between you and Ug, Mug, Bug, Pug, Gug, Chug, Trevor, Rachel and Timothy, you would swap the fourth leg for a chariot. When you had collected three chariots you could swap the one you didn't need to keep up with the Ogs next door for a television video game or a lucky mammoth's tusk.

If you had no spear and couldn't go out and kill something with four legs you could either be a vegetarian or go and borrow a spear from a bank, for which you'd have to put up your cave as security or, if it was a council cave you were living in or a rented cave, you'd have to go to a spear-lender. If you didn't want to borrow a spear you could go to a finance company and ask them to float you in business with a couple of legs. If they refused, you wouldn't have a leg to stand on.

Supposing you carried on a fair barter in legs and chariots and such like and eventually ended up with two television video games and a couple of spare legs. The spare legs could be swapped for a couple of seats for the Solstice. One of the seats for the Solstice could be swapped for a tin of liver salts which would come in handy after all that mead and woad and nuts and berries at Beltane.

Then an enterprising pre-numismatic Neanderthaler had a bright idea and thereby introduced much misery into the world. He invented investing. 'If you've got any spare legs or chariots or things then lend them me,' he said, 'and I'll lend them to somebody else to set up factories to make more legs and chariots and things' – thereby introducing employment and his mate, unemployment, on to the scene as well. Soon the early Stock Exchange at Cerne Abbas rang to the shouts of jobbers selling stocks and shares in Consolidated Woad and International Torques.

At the same time, of course, the enterprising Neanderthaler also invented inflation because since the possession of things meant the Good Life – and everybody wanted the Good Life – they all started to charge more for their services and things. The price of chariots went up to six legs so the hunters changed the exchange rate on legs to four axe heads instead of two. The torque business, unable to compete went bust and the torque-makers signed on the dole. The chiefs wanted to cut back public spending on chariotways, the dole and sick caves in an attempt to force back the amount of legs and chariots on the market and therefore keep down prices. This threw the chariot-builders out of work, the chariotway-builders and the men who minded the sick caves. Not only were they on the dole, they were not making anything and were therefore twice the drain on the economy they should have been. Confidence in the market fell and woad works closed down as share selling hit a feverish high. Hundreds of investors jumped off Stonehenge in the great crash.

This was the First Capitalist Crisis.

Because legs, chariots, pots of woad and torques were bulky to store and hard to get in your pocket it became necessary to invent money. At first money was made of mud and feathers or ox dung, but every time it rained the money melted and people went bankrupt. Then people tried using mammoth legs as legal tender but some of the legs weren't tender, in fact, they were very tough and what was worse they went off in hot weather and people got rid of them so there would be a run on legs, followed by a run on liver salts, followed by a run generally.

Another thing about legs, mud, feathers and stones was that they were easy to forge so men started making money out of harder things like drunkards' livers and second-hand chariot salesmen's hearts. Then, with the discovery of coining, the Age of Capitalism really got under way.

The first coins were pieces of gold 14 feet across, 12 feet tall and two inches deep. They proved impractical because people had to have pockets in their trousers the size of tents and the slot machines at Avebury Fun Fair were too big to use. Also it was hard to get any change for them since the supply of seven feet coins and three-and-a-half feet coins was limited.

Then someone got the idea of making them very small and calling them just as valuable. A practice still carried out by present-day governments.

So that people would know which tribe used which coins, they decided to put a picture on the front. In those days people believed that a man's soul could be taken away in his likeness so the only one that would agree to have his picture on the front was the village idiot. In the course of time, as money became more important, so, by association, did the village idiot – a fact which accounts for the emergence of the monarchy almost as well as the robber baron theory does.

MOTOR CARS

Poop poop   TOAD OF TOAD HALL

You can have any colour so long as it's green   HENRY FROG

After thousands of years of civilization – from the discovery that a sawn-off bit of log would roll downhill, and that two sawn-off bits of log with an axle in between would roll downhill in a straight line, and the final realization that two sawn-off log ends and an axle could be fastened to a box and would allow someone to drive it downhill very fast, running over people and killing them – mankind has evolved into being the keeper of and slave to the motor car.

The research plants of Coventry, Detroit and Turin have spent many millions of pounds developing a machine that propels itself on the distilled bodies of long dead animals into crowds of other machines on networks of concrete highways that have blighted the landscape and are as clogged as the arteries of an overweight company executive.

Let's examine the motor car and its effects in a little detail. First, some common fallacies.

1 'It gets you from A to B'

It does not get you from A to B because
- a) the council has just dug the sewers up again
- b) a 42-ton juggernaut has just shed its load of dried Westphalian goat curd across both carriageways of the M1 near Mexborough
- c) everybody in A has decided to go to B at the same time and there is a 12-mile tailback

Even if you get to B the cafés are full, the ice cream costs more than a night out did in 1946, it's raining, the sea's full

129

of sewage and the dog has thrown up on the sandwiches on the back seat.

2 'Cars are a convenience'

I would agree with this statement only in the cloacal sense of the word 'convenience'. Cars are an inconvenience. The minute you get them they start rusting faster then they can depreciate. They cannot get you from door to door because you're not allowed to park there. You have to park a mile away from the door you're going to and walk the rest of the way. And because you're in the car, you didn't bring any rainwear and it is, of course, raining, so you get soaked.

John Donne was nearer the truth than he'll ever know when he said 'No man is an island'. Nowhere is that more true than in traffic when every man gets in every other man's way and when men suddenly become aware of how small this planet is and how equal we all are in the traffic snarl-up. Nowhere is there a more democratic meeting-place than the tarmac ribbons of the land. Wealthy Arabs in Rolls-Royces are bumper to bumper with builders' merchants in clapped-out lorries, while alongside them a headmaster shakes his fist at a burglar in a Jaguar, while across the way a massage parlour lady is giving the V-sign to a mini-van full of nuns. Nowhere in the world do the high born and the low bred, the rich and the behind-on-the-payments rub bumpers on such equal footing.

In truth your car inconveniences every other car on the road, just as all the other cars on the road inconvenience you. If you are going slowly in front of him, he flashes you, honks at you and, foot jammed down on the pedal, he passes you glaring and gesticulating. Only if you're lucky does he run into the back of a police car. If he is going slowly in front of you, your blood pressure rises, you grit your teeth and clench the steering wheel aggressively,

NOW, NOW, SIR...NO MAN IS A TRAFFIC ISLAND!

muttering maledictions and likening the culprit to repro-
ductional appendages and instruments for infantile
nourishment. The adrenalin forces your heart rate up, the
lumps of cholesterol are prowling through your arteries
towards your aorta like force-fed slugs. Then as you snarl
past him with your engine shaking itself free of piston
rings and gaskets, waving your fist violently, you discover
that you are passing your doctor and his wife who are just
out for a Sunday run; so that later, when you do have your
coronary, he is very late getting there.

3 'It's a good way of seeing the countryside'

In all the years I spent as a pro-musician travelling the
length and breadth of the British Isles I saw no more of the
countryside than you would do looking at a big television
screen. The only time I really saw the countryside was
when I got off my backside and walked away from the car
and looked around me. You see nothing from the inside of
a car except other cars flashing past or the occasional big

thing like a mountain or very close cow. Everything is reduced to the scale of the windscreen.

Worst Saying Ever Heard in a Car

Thirty-odd-year-old woman to husband in car with windows wound down in Lake District overlooking Ullswater: 'In tit lovely, just like a photograph!'

I'm haunted by the vision of people who spend their Sundays driving to the seaside or what we have left of the countryside where they park their cars and sit inside reading their papers with the radio on, the window half down and gran and the yapping poodle on the back seat. They stare out glumly, trapped in their heavily financed metal wombs, terrified of leaving them and getting their nice Sunday clothes messed up, feeling in some way that they should be enjoying themselves.

The motor car is dirty, noisy, inefficient, built only to fall apart. It uses too much and too many of the earth's resources and has been instrumental in the destruction of most of our cities. It is second only to heavy transport and the road transport lobby in the destruction of our country-side and it has killed more people than two world wars.

Apart from that, there is nothing wrong with it.

Another thing that flummoxes me about the motor car is the way some people use it to drive to a lay-by on a major trunk road like the A1 for a picnic.

The car is usually a smallish family saloon, the occu-pants middle aged. A couple, usually with a gran or two get out and unfold a picnic table, chairs, cutlery, plates, condiments, cups and saucers and tupperware boxes of food. They light the camping gaz stove and put the whistling kettle on. They turn on the portable radio and start to eat as juggernauts scream past, their slipstream sending the boiled ham flapping off the plates like a flock of manic pink bats. All three fall asleep after tea and gran sleepwalks under a passing juggernaut.

Is that what these people are? Some sort of euthenasia squad. Acme Euthenasia Company: our motto – IF THE WAGONS DON'T GET YOU THE DIESEL FUMES WILL.

MOVING HOUSE

Try not to do it. You will become involved with estate agents, lawyers, bank managers and removal men all of whom make Jack the Ripper look like Noddy. You can kiss goodbye to your nerves, your peace of mind and most of your money and say hello to a house that, though it once seemed the bijou castle of your birthright, now, in a space of days, has mysteriously sprouted dry rot, falling window panes, blocked lavatory pans, repeatedly fusing lights and doors that either don't shut or only do so when you pull them so hard the edifice shakes to its foundations.

The worst thing about moving house is the chain.

This happens when the people buying your house are selling theirs to someone who's trying to sell his; while the people who are selling you theirs are waiting to move into the house they're moving to while the people who are selling them theirs are waiting for the people whose house they are buying to move out. At one end of the chain is the Pope and at the other a yak butter fuel stove maker in Ulan Bator.

Don't buy a house from anyone called Usher.

MUSIC

If music be the food of love, why don't rabbits play banjoes?
M. HARDING

Music helps to take my mind off things NERO

Music, the most universal of the arts after dominoes and grass flattening is an international language. Music, like the trade winds, travels the globe from West to East and in Japan they now play the violin at the drop of a kimono. Yet how many people in Wolverhampton, you ask, play the kyoto? And I am forced to answer, not a solitary one.

As an Anarchist your problems, musicwise, are likely to fall into one or all of the following categories: insistence of parent on desirability of musical education; musak; inability to rise at national anthem.

Taking them one at a time.

If you don't want to learn a musical instrument and your parents insist, choose something diabolical like the Columbian ear trumpet, the Maori nose harp or the Guatemalian shoe horn. Not only will they be hard put to find a teacher for obscure instruments like these but, if you manage to play them badly enough, you should be able to put them off forcing a tuneful or percussive education on you for life.

Musak, together with personal membrane itching and television video games, is actually the ninth plague that God inflicted on the Egyptians and hence on the rest of the world. Music is like sex, there should be a build-up and awakening of interest leading to some sort of involvement and ultimately, if you are lucky, to some sort of a conclusion or climax. The unending drivel that pours from self-repeating tape loops joined to boxes hidden in the ceilings of airports, bars, barbers, chip chops, cafés, department stores and even public urinals is an insult not just to composers and musicians, living and dead, but to anyone who's ever wanted to buy a fountain pen or have a crap in peace without a ninth rate version of *Begin the Beguine* slurping round his ears like a trail of treacle.

I have heard first-hand accounts of musak recording sessions, horrifying stories of musicians playing for hours on end in basement studios fortified only by crates of whisky and endless cigarettes working their way through every decent and not-so-decent combination of musical notes ever devised. You would not treat an animal so.

National anthems are stupid things, too. They represent nationalism at its worst pitch. If you don't believe in either God or Queens then why should you stand up for either of them – particularly since neither has done very much for you? The Anarchists' anthem is an international anthem that consists of 365 raspberries blown in very quick succession to the tune of Camptown races. Nobody has to stand up for it, nobody has to listen to it and, even better, nobody has to play it.

NORWICH

The people of Norwich in 1926, hearing of Parkinson's disease for the first time, shot everybody in the town of that name.

ORGIES _____

To have an orgy you have to have an orgist and some orgisters, the more the merrier. Try and arrange to have the heating on and a bit of refreshment for half-time.

If it's an open-air do, tear down some of the park railings and roast a swan. Keep out of nettle beds and meadows where cows have been recently.

If it is an indoor orgy, try and make sure that everybody knows that they're at an orgy. There's nothing worse than flinging off your duffle coat and wranglers and shouting, 'Right, let's get down to it' just to find that the rest of the people in the room think it's a tupperware party.

PANDANGA _____

The Ruffled Padanga of Borneo and Rotherham spreads out his feathers in his courtship dance and imitates Winston Churchill and Tommy Cooper on one leg. The padanga is dying out because the female padanga doesn't take it too seriously.

PARENTS _____

Nothing to get cut up about   LIZZIE BORDEN

I'd walk a million miles for one of your smiles   OEDIPUS

Parents, like marriage, children and babies, are part of the trap that Nature has devised to ensure the continuation of our species. Observe the scorpion who lugs her offspring about on her back for umpteen weeks until they are big enough to hurt people on their own and think how similar is the relationship between human parents and their young.

The jackals of Africa teach their cubs to hunt and kill with the same single-minded ferocity and cunning that the upper classes still use in finding mates for their sons and daughters. The lie that Nature cheats us with is that parental love, unselfish and freely given, is rewarded by filial affection. Cobblers. The universal complaint amongst elderly parents is, 'My children never come to see me'.

The only answer to that is don't have any children in the first place; and if you've got them, don't let them out of your sight – follow them everywhere; don't let them move house without you; don't go on any long journeys without making sure they won't have moved away by the time you get back.

Children and parents spend most of their lives not understanding each other and the rest of their lives not wanting to see each other. What amazes me is why we do it. I can only put it down, as I said at the beginning to an atavistic instinct for continuation. Either that or Dr Spock is in the pay of the Martians.

PARTIES

I love parties!   BANQUO
Parties are the best way to lose friends   LUCREZIA BORGIA
More dust, Pip?   MISS HAVERSHAM

The Armchair Anarchist knows in his very marrow that parties are impossible affairs. Mark Hiding described them as 'the unspeakable meeting the unloveable surrounded by the uneatable, the undrinkable and the unthinkable'.

Most Anarchists know that parties run pretty much to form. You learn this at the very first party you go to, which is usually a birthday party for some kid you know at nursery. The host kid gets the most of everything, gets to kiss all the girls/boys, stabs you in the ear with a cheese finger, throws up on you, pours lemonade down your pants and tells everyone you've wet yourself, and then gets you sent home by saying that you just asked him/her to show you his/her knickers/willy.

Be warned: but as Casanova said, 'Hope beats eternal in the human trousers.' Armed with this knowledge and very little else, the average adolescent spends a lot of weekends going to, giving and organizing parties.

Adolescent parties

At adolescent parties people run round a lot and giggle. There is much heavy breathing, scratching of records and tears in bathrooms. The garden is usually full of young bloods fresh from the rigours of O-Level Sociology bringing back their first bellyful of cider and cooking sherry all over your prize brassicas. Someone usually breaks Wedgwood at this kind of do and hides it in a cushion. For years you wonder where the bon bon dish or the vase has gone and why every time you sit back on the settee you end up with a lacerated back. They usually do something to the dog that ends up with its skulking in the airing cupboard for months biting anybody who looks remotely like Kevin Keegan. People can also get pregnant at these parties.

The best way to avoid most of these things is to paint a large white cross on the door and arrange for black-caped men with bells ringing to wander round the block a couple of times or three.

To prevent pregnancies arrange for the water cistern to be filled with bromide and for large frequent explosions to take place every so often.

Showbiz parties

Should be avoided unless you can watch 300 acts at the same time.

Trendy parties

Stick a five pound note up each nostril and pretend that you're as blocked as everybody else. NB That's not talcum powder they're sniffing up those fivers.

Professional people's parties

Try not to notice the hair transplants, silicone tits that don't match and the face lifts that have given the owners a permanent manic grin. At one of these parties someone will be sure to try and sell you insurance. The best ploy is to fall down frothing at the mouth and arrange to be carried home.

PHILOSOPHY

The art of finding answers for questions that haven't been asked ERIC DOPPELGANGER

Philosophers are charlatans who make their money by going around making up bogus questions about things to which there is no real answer, e.g. 'What is the meaning of meaning?', 'What is being?', 'What is time?' when everybody knows that the only questions that people really want to know the answers to are questions like 'What will win the 3.30 at Haydock tomorrow?' and 'Will Auntie Vera stay for a fortnight or a week this year?' and 'What will the weather be like in November because I want to fix up my holidays?' The Oracle at Delphi was never asked questions like 'What is truth, what is beauty?' but instead was deluged with questions about how to get wine stains off chiffons, how to grow trees from avocado pears and how to make slaves fall in love with you; which is why the oracle got fed up in the end and went off somewhere else.

PLAGUES _____

Plagues are usually haphazard and you probably won't know you've got one until you break out in locusts or frogs or dead first-borns. Plagues were invented by Moses to get his people out of Egypt in 4,000 B.C. on a Friday afternoon. The worst plagues are plagues of frogs because they move about a lot more than boils or plagues of personal membrane itching (the plague that finally made Pharoah give in). Plagues of frogs can be cured by storks but this can in itself be dangerous, since storks aren't all that careful where they peck.

If a plague breaks out near you, e.g. frogs

1 phone the fire brigade
2 stay indoors until it's all over
3 don't open any letters that hop

POLICEMEN _____

All right you two, come quietly POLICEMAN TO DEAF MUTE
COUPLE HAVING IT OFF IN A CAR

Example of policeman telling joke:

'A man was perambulating in a certain direction at a certain time when he had cause to enter a premises licensed for medical practice where he wished to avail himself of the services of a qualified physician. The man approached the medical practitioner in a patient-like fashion and told him, the physician that is, that his hair was falling out. He further had occasion to ask the doctor if he could give him anything to keep it in whereupon the doctor gave him a container of the cardboard sort normally used for keeping other things in such as tins of domestic furniture polish.'

All policemen have a special operation when they join the force. It's a simple operation consisting of a small nick in the cheeks and a couple of stitches that gives them a permanent 'I'm not having that one, sir' grin.

The Armchair Anarchist and the police

Try and avoid them; don't ask one the time without seeing your lawyer first; and if a policeman tries to speak to you
1 phone the fire brigade
2 run

PROMETHEUS, ERIC J._____

Second-hand car salesman and visionary. Wrote several mystical books on leylines, spirals, dowsing and ash-tray reading. A world-wide expert on parasites on man (e.g. insurance companies and banks) he died in 1934 while trying to read his own entrails. Some of his words of wisdom were recorded by his lover, Rover.

'If I wasn't here I'd be somewhere else.' (Dowsing for the Deaf)

'All around me is nothing and all I hear is the rumbling of muted fools.'
(Tory Party Conferences as an aid to Transcendental Materialism)

QUIM, FRED

Fred Quim from Walthamstow ate nothing for 14 years but wood because he believed that, by doing so, he would take on the properties of the trees that the wood came from (oak – strength, willow – sensitivity, hawthorn – resilience etc.). He contracted Dutch Elm disease and died in 1974 when he was blown down in a winter gale. An autopsy revealed that he had lied when he stated his age to be 67 since the pathologist who examined him found 76 rings in his trunk.

RAIL TRAVEL

Rail travel was invented by Mad Eric the Druid, the man who designed and built the Stonehenge to Woodhenge overhead line which ran successfully until it was nationalized in 57 B.C. Immediately private transporters switched over to ox-powered chariots and started building oxcart ways. The overhead railway folded, although some of the lines are still standing (e.g. Stonehenge turntable). Rail travel was then forgotten about for many thousands of years and many people died at stations waiting for trains that never came. Stephenson reintroduced rail travel and thus started the Industrial Revolution when an interplanetary vehicle he had invented failed to achieve take-off

MY GOD, HUBERT... THE CATS GOT THE KETTLE!

speed and instead became a colliery engine running between Stockton and Darlington.

Thus began the Age of Steam.

Steam founded the British Empire (and we all know what happened to that), the British Navy, the skyscrapers of New York, Chinese laundries and whistling kettles (which soon replaced canaries in most homes).

Rail travel should be one of the pleasantest ways of getting about and in fact I'd rather go by train than by car any day since being sandwiched between juggernauts on the M1 in the fog at 70 m.p.h. is not my idea of how to get about. In Britain, however, the railways seem to be run by people determined to show that nationalization will never work. From the station floor to the head of British Rail there seems to be an attitude and an atmosphere of hopeless cockedupness. Thirty porters stand around looking as though they've just picked their uniforms up from under a heap of coke, while passengers wobble all over the station under mountains of suitcases looking for luggage trolleys, and all the luggage trolleys are hidden under a heap of mailbags that have been there a week and a half.

If you have to go by British Rail, face facts. It will probably be late leaving and arriving. The buffet car, if there is one at all, will serve grey coffee, sandwiches designed by Andy Warhol and if you're lucky you'll be able to take out a mortgage on a pie that a tortoise would be happy to make a home in.

If a British Rail pie bites you, take it back and complain. British Rail gravy is specially made to stay on your plate even if trains turn upside down. This gravy has been specially developed at the British Rail food research centre at Fakenham where they have also developed indestructable reusable pie crusts and long-life sandwiches made from crushed alabaster sandwiches of St Pancreas the patron saint of dyspeptics and rail travellers.

RELIGION _____

Religion has been the death of a lot of people, e.g. Latimer and Ridley, Joan of Arc, the Huguenots and God Jun. More wars have been fought in the name of religion than for any other single cause unless you are thinking of the wars that have been fought over kids kicking their balls into the next door neighbour's garden.

With so many religions claiming to be the one true path to salvation, it can be confusing to the atheist, agnostic or simply the mystified person to contemplate how people who don't eat pork and are circumcised can possibly go to the same paradise as people who put bones through their noses and eat each other.*

But more confusing still is the fact that religious denominations worshipping a man called Jesus Christ are prepared to bomb, torture and revile each other in his name in Northern Ireland. The Armchair Anarchist is usually also an armchair (or closet) atheist or at the least has very strong doubts.

The following is a list of some of the better known and some of the more obscure religions. If anybody is offended by references to their own religion which they feel to be mocking or derisory can I just point out that there will be a lot of other religions getting a bit of stick and not just yours.

Botulism

Founded by St Ernest Bot, the man who discovered Navel Fluff. Bot was born in Swindon in 1846, the product of an

---

*The answer, some would say, is that they don't.

overnight liaison between a downstairs maid called Chastity Perdue and a self-styled 'Doctor' Jim Bot, a one-armed Punch and Judy man who did a very novel show. Bot was a mystic and faith-healer who, at the laying on of hands that took place with Chastity Perdue who had gone to him to be cured of a limp caused by a falling ironing board, cured her by taking the ironing board out of her shoe. She was so grateful she gave her body to him, but it didn't fit.

And so the fruit of their loins was sprung forth upon the world mewling and puking on to this mortal coil, as Biggles once said, or was it Dan Dare?

The young Bot, who was christened Ernest, inherited from his father the gift of seeing into the future, only three-thousandths of a second into the future admittedly, but it did enable him to dodge bullets and knives which is how he came to be working as Unlucky Leon the Knife Thrower's ninety-seventh assistant.

On his eightieth birthday, having outlived Unlucky Leon, he went to live in a cave in the superstructure of the old scenic railway on Blackpool's pleasure beach where he soon became a major tourist attraction.

He dedicated what was left of his life to a search for inner knowledge. For hours without end he sat outside the mouth of his plaster of paris and chicken-wire cave contemplating his navel, oblivious of the hooting crowds that were pelting him with old candyfloss sticks, orange peel and invitations to speak at Masonic and Rotary Club dinners.

It was on a hot August bank holiday Monday that Bot discovered navel fluff while contemplating that very same spot. At first he considered it might have been a stray bit of candy floss and tried to pick it out with a hat pin a lady had once stuck in him on a crowded tram when a German sausage he was taking home for his aged mother had got pushed against the lady in the crush.

When he discovered that the detritus in his navel was not candy floss but fluff accumulated over many years, he realized that man's inability to see deep within himself was caused not by any lack of meditative training but by great wads of navel fluff blocking the way to inner knowledge.

Followers of Botulism* wear glass navel plugs and visit the crazy golf course at Lytham St Annes once a year where Bot is buried under the little toadstool with the red top with white dots on it. Bot's cave on the scenic railway was destroyed when the railway was closed to make room for the Feelerama – Superspinner – Roller – Disco – Skateboard – Hulla – Hoop – Space – Odyssey – Guaranteed – Throw – Up – Golden – Pancake – Waffle – Ride.

British Israelites

The British Israelites believe the white Anglo-Saxons of Britain to be descended from the ten lost tribes of Israel deported by Sargon of Assyria on the fall of Sumaria in 721 B.C.

They also believe that Dick Barton and Muffin the Mule were one and the same person and that if you tread on a nick you'll marry a brick and a beetle will come to your wedding. They further believe that the future can be foretold by the measurements of the Great Pyramid which probably means it will be big and yellow and in the hands of the Arabs. They also believe that if you sleep with your head under the pillow a fairy will come and take all your teeth.

Cargo Cult

This religion is found in various of the islands which make up Melanesia. It is based on a belief common to primitive

*There are 137 of them.

peoples which linked the religion of any new or foreign arrivals with the goods they carried with them. So, by embracing the strangers' religion, the natives believed that they would also get the knives, axes and other western artefacts that the missionaries brought with them. Cargo cults were further strengthened by the arrival of the Americans to fight the Japanese in 1942 and now the followers of the religion drill with bamboo rifles and talk into empty beer cans. They await the coming of a saviour called John Frum who is an American and lives in a volcano on one of the islands. John Frum, it is said, is a small man with bleached hair, a high-pitched voice and shiny buttons. He, when he comes, will arrive in a four-engined plane and at the coming of Frum there will be no end to the cargo that will come with him in the great airlift.

Before we laugh too loudly at these Melanesians, think how strange Christianity would seem to them where the Second Coming would bring with it only the separation of men's souls from their bodies and a unification with a Great Being in a mythical location beyond tax inspectors or politicians called Paradise. At least the Melanesians know what a plane looks like. The only thing most Christians agree upon is that God has a long white beard and the angels have bare feet, white nighties and swans' wings. All in all, Frum is beginning to sound quite a plausable character. At least they know what his voice sounds like.

Druidism

Druidism consists largely in collecting mistletoe with golden sickles and waiting for solstices. Quite a good religion that doesn't take up a lot of time and hasn't caused many wars since Roman times. Recommended for people

who don't mind standing on moors in the rain and the dark
and who like wearing white nighties and being laughed at.

Nihilism

Nihilism is probably the best religion of all for Anarchists
to follow. St Nihil was the son of Madoc, the Welsh king,
the Blodwyn Phwyllgrndog, the Abbess of Llanddgrid-
phywll.

He was a quiet boy and nobody thought he had the
makings of a saint until he was 13 and it was discovered
that he had no interest in rugby, choral singing or beer. He
was tortured for his apostasy, and for four years he was
buried alive in a vat of laver bread and beaten with
parboiled leeks, but still refused to admit that rugby,
choral singing and beer were necessary for salvation. His
heart is buried in Llandofmeifadas and has become a
Nihilist shrine.

Nihilism consists basically in doing nothing that you
don't want to do and, if forced to do it, you do it badly.

Pope Goestheveezl

Pope Goestheveezl was the shortest reigning pope in the
history of the Church, reigning for two hours and six
minutes on 1 April 1866. The white smoke had hardly
faded into the blue of the Vatican skies before it dawned
on the assembled multitudes in St Peter's Square that his
name had hilarious possibilities. The crowds fell about,
helpless with laughter, singing

Half a pound of tuppeny rice
Half a pound of treacle
That's the way the chimney smokes
Pope Goestheveezl

BE SERIOUS, LADS... LET'S GIVE THE JOB TO POPE SIKOLA!

The square was finally cleared by armed carabineri with tears of laughter streaming down their faces. The event set a record for hilarious civic functions smashing the previous record set when Baron Hans Neizant Bömpzidaizi was elected Landburgher of Köln in 1653.

RELIGONS THAT KNOCK ON YOUR DOOR

Jehovah's Witnesses

Say you never saw the accident and he's a lousy driver anyway (*see* Eric von Waniker)

Mormons

Mormons believe that an angel called Moroney came to earth and gave a man called Joseph Smith some gold plates on which was written the Book of Mormon. The writing could be read only with special emerald glasses which the angel just happened to have with him. Smith went behind a blanket and shouted out the Book of Mormon over the top of the blanket while some friends who had never seen the plates or the glasses or the angel wrote it all down. And all the time nobody laughed.

Mormons don't drink or smoke but they can have a lot of wives so they probably need all their energy. They also believe that the ten tribes of Israel ended up in America so that between the Mormons and the British Israelites those tribes must have done a lot of swimming.

If crew-cut young men in business suits knock on your door, tell them that you're Jewish and that all your money goes to Salt Beef City.

Encyclopedia salesmen

Invite them all in. Nip out the back door. Phone the police and tell them your house is being burgled.

Rent men

A religious sect that knock on your door and shout maledictions on the people inside such as, 'Ah know yer in'.

St Elmo's Fire

This is an inflamation of the externum of the lower intestinal tract also known as the Squitters, the Trotters, the Aztec Two-Step and Gandhi's Revenge; it is an ailment common to frequenters of curry houses or people on package holidays to unsavoury climes. Sufferers of the fire can be recognized by their red eyes, mournful expression and tendency to stand during long bus journeys on bad roads. A characteristic St Elmo's Whimper can also be heard from time to time.

St Elmo, who is the patron saint of underwear makers, was martyred in Rangoon in 1726. He was a Benedictine friar who died while trying to learn the secret of Goolie Bajia at the head of the Irrawaddi. The general opinion is that it served him right.

Saint Sbury

Patron saint of viand merchants and cheese-makers, Saint Sbury walked barefoot over a bed of scalding hot meat pies at York in A.D. 423 and was martyred to death on a bacon slicer in St Albans Co-Op in 467.

SELF DEFENCE

Koh-I-Matsu

The Japanese art of bad breath. Defence against a would-be attacker is perfected after long years of eating nothing but garlic, pickled onions, asafoetida and British Rail pies. Adepts of Koh-I-Matsu can blind an opponent at 40 yards.

Kam-Sitsu

The art of thinking that nothing is happening to you while you are being beaten to death.

Yan-Kyo-Tying

The art of ripping the heads off daisies with your eyelids.

Foo-Hyook

Teaches you how to reduce a 20-stone opponent to a gibbering wreck fit for nothing but macramé, by singing old Vera Lynn songs and reciting Tennyson's *Morte D'Arthur* in a Birmingham accent.

Ch'i Hing

The art of mystifying your opponent by reciting the names of all the Chinese takeaways within a 12-mile radius of Liverpool's Pier Head. The practitioner can usually get one or more opponents arguing about the numbers and locations of the Chinese takeaways while he does a bunk. In Glasgow the same thing works with the names of bars.

SEX

Stop it or you'll go blind MRS HOMER

I'm coming SNOW WHITE

So am I, so am I, so am I, so am I, so am I, so am I, wait for me, my shoe's come off SEVEN DWARFS

Sex is like food – out of doors the biggest problem is the flies ERIC CARRIER

Lie back and think of a number between one and ten QUEEN VICTORIA TO HER DAUGHTER

All true Armchair Anarchists recognize that there is something inherently comic in the sexual act. It consists largely of a combination of ludicrous physical movements in a confined space with a conjoining of remote areas of the body usually reserved for other functions. This is accompanied by a rise in blood pressure and a shouting of unintelligible phrases during which the movements get faster and more erratic until they suddenly stop.

At one time, far back in the primordial mists of history, mankind reproduced by cross-pollination and sex was thus the job of the birds and the bees and the sablehair brush. Alternatively, people were grafted on to each other. Evidence of grafting can be found in the totem poles of the North American Indians, particularly among the Sioux, who grafted men on to eagles in an attempt to cut down on postage charges and bus fares.

Sex was discovered first of all in a roundabout way by Onan who fell over, grabbed on to himself, liked it and kept hold. Realizing that he had cornered the market in a new form of home entertainment, he tried to patent the idea but, unfortunately for Onan, most of the people around had the necessary tackle. So Onan went away and invented television video games instead. The idea spread and all over people fell over and held on to themselves until, in a crowded passage in one of the pyramids so narrow everyone walked sideways, two passing Onanists bumped into each other in the dark and discovered sex as we know it.

Once sex was discovered, Man went in for it in a big way and, in fact, spent most of his time in caves doing it. It was for this reason that he completely missed the Ice Age. The Ice Age killed off all the mammoths and the eohippo and hot dog salesmen so that when the first men and women came out of the caves several stone lighter looking for brown ale and oysters, they had to start growing things so that they could eat. This meant that Man had to work for a living. This gave men less time for sex and introduced the dilemma that has been with us through the ages, named after its discoverer, Uglic, the Red-eyed; Uglic's First Law of Sexual Economics states: 'The more you work for it, the less time you have to do it'.

163

SEXUAL CUSTOMS OF OTHER LANDS___

Mesopotamia

In Mesopotamia it is immoral to expose the nose or index finger to the common view. They are always kept well covered in accordance with the laws laid down by Eric Hammurabi the Sun God. (Laws Vol VI Part II, a bi-monthly link House publication.)

'Yea, thou shalt keep covered thy nostrils and thy index finger in case thou inflamest thy neighbour's loins or his goat or his city gates.'

Anyone found picking their nose in Mesopotamia is thought to be having sex in public and is beaten with a sack of old *National Geographic* magazines until he or she has a nosebleed or shouts 'Ballies!!' or 'I give in'.

Arabia

A woman taken in adultery in Arabia is put in a leather bag and swung against a wall. The penalty for reading *Playgirl* is doing the washing up for a week.

Easter Island

The men of Easter Island wear penile sheaths made from rolled up copies of *Old Moore's Almanac* topped off with papier maché monster heads to ward off evil spirits.

On high days and holy days and on other days as well the men prance about waving them in the air shouting, 'Wanna gdunga fella waiku waiku'. The women merely laugh and drink themselves senseless leaving the men to go off muttering with sexual frustration which they relieve only by building huge stone statues of men with long faces staring miserably out to sea. And so would you.

SEXUAL POSITIONS

Q How do you stand on the Russian position?
A You don't – you kneel on a bearskin rug.

Missionary – Two plane tickets to Africa and a map of Mungo Park's travels

Doggie Fashion – Look at pictures of lamp-posts while eating charcoal biscuits and pin blue rosettes on each other

Silly Joke
'Let's try the missionary position'
'I'm not climbing in that cooking pot for anyone'

There are something like 70,000 spermatozoa released in every sexual act. Only one makes it to the uterus. The rest shrug their shoulders and wander off looking for something else to do.

SEXUAL TERMS
A glossary

Cunnilingus   Clever Irish airlines

Felatio   Character in one of Shakespeare's lost
plays, *Two Gents in Venerea*. The lover
of Pudenda, Felatio is one of the two
gentlemen of the title. Scrotum, a
wrinkled retainer, and Prepuce, a mal-
content, attempt to seduce Pudenda
and Labia, her serving-maid; Felatio
and his companion, Coitus Interrup-
tus, manage to thwart their plans.

Fetishism   Fetishists are followers of Hitler and
Mussolini; they are also people who
collect things that they associate with
sexual arousal, e.g. shoes, panties,
money. Even stranger fetishists are
people who collect beetles, dinky cars,
butterflies and train numbers. The lat-
ter can be seen most Sunday mornings
on station platforms – they dress in
raincoats and carry wet notebooks and
binoculars. When certain trains come
into view, they reach a sexual climax,
running up and down the platform
waving their notebooks and leaping in
the air, shouting, 'It's coming, it's
coming, it's a Deltic, it's a Deltic', until
the train has gone past when they settle
down again in their wet raincoats or

slink off for a post-orgasmic BR pie and mug of brown.

Homosexuality	Now no longer regarded as a deviation, it is in fact compulsory in some professions, e.g. spies, liberal party, lady mud wrestlers. Many famous people have been homosexuals – Leonardo da Vinci, Eric, Oscar Wilde, Quentin Crisp, Michelangelo. Michelangelo painted the Sistine Chapel lying on his back because he didn't trust the other workmen.
Masochism	Masochists like being tied to chairs and hit.
Nasal sex	Eskimos
Oral Roberts	An American preacher who doesn't talk about it.
Oral sex	Talking about it, e.g. 'Your place or mine?'
Sadism	Sadists are people who like tying people to chairs and hitting them. Together with masochists, they account for the relationship between criminals and the police.
Sex in schools	Behind the bike shed is the usual place.
69	Sex is still possible at this age.

Some more notes on sex

So much emphasis is put on sex nowadays that we may indeed end up with Sex Olympics. The Russians would be in training for years, the Americans would offer college courses and degrees to anyone who showed any promise at it and the British would have talented plumbers and dental receptionists doing it in their dinner-hour at work.

The arena would be crowded with people and the judges would hold up cards with 5.6., 6.2., 3.5 and 4.9 on them. The commentary broadcast live all over the world would be something like – 'He's coming in to finish now. Is this going to be Britain's first gold? He's been doing so well recently particularly in the empire pool at Wembley when he managed 24 air-hostesses and a lady school crossing attendant in 4 hours 27 minutes. That was Britain's first under-five this year. And now is he going to do it, it's very close. No! The postman's knocked and the kids have started fighting downstairs. Oh bad luck! The Russians have got it again.'

Books on sex

These can give you a terrible inferiority complex and make you feel as though all your life you've been a non-starter in an affair that is about as natural as blowing your nose though much more exciting.

They show positions for coitus that it would take an Indian mystic a lifetime to achieve and still leave you with no one to talk to.

The scene: a bedroom. Cast: a couple naked and un-accoutred save for a large book, *The World Encyclopedia of Sexual Positions*.
Man Right, Betty, lift your leg up and put it behind your neck. Good. Now I'll just stand on this egg box. Right. I've got to lean over and get my arm up between your knee and my ear. That's it. Now you put your elbow behind my left ankle and I put my foot through the gap between your

right knee and your left elbow. Hang on I can't move. You move. What do you mean you can't? We can't be stuck. Bloody Hell we are.

Rover! Now get down Rover, stop it, go away, Rover. If I get free from this I'll kill you, Rover. Pack it in. Get down.

SMALL CHILDREN

Small children go for your shins. They have toys that go for your shins, they have pushalong, walkerbuggies that can all but sever your radius and when they've raised enough lumps on your shins, they use them as stepping-stones to climb up on your knee.

What to do

If they're your own children, there's not a lot you can do. If they belong to someone else, sneer malevolently every time they come near you, show them stills from *The Massacre of the Innocents* and let joke blood dribble from your lips.

SMITH, ADAM

Smith wrote the *Wealth of Nations* and thereby brought about the self-justification of monetarism, a creed which didn't work then (particularly if you were a little boy chimney sweep) and doesn't work now.

STEP PYRAMIDS

These were built to discourage door-to-door salesmen. Their success accounts for the dearth of travelling salesmen jokes in Egypt and Mexico and the strange names they gave each other (e.g. Amenhotep, Quetzalcoatl) in order to have something to laugh at.

TELEVISION_____

'So now let's meet the first of our contestants who's going to let me make a fool of him in front of twelve million people because he knows that at the end of it he still gets all his expenses paid and a consolation prize worth £300 even if he cocks it all up and doesn't get a single question right . . . So here he is the first contender this week in our *"How to let bits of your life sink away into oblivion in half-hour pieces broken up only by cretinous commercials Quiz . . ."* Here he is, a taxi driver who works on the London Airport run, he lives in a penthouse in Knightsbridge and in his spare time collects books on Hopi Rain Dancers . . . Mr Sid Bingo.' (Cue applause, cue music, enter contestant) *The Eric Mindrot Show*.

Television has become the universal medium and what is also true about it is that it is universally bad. It is the mindless Punch and Judy show in the corner of the hut that shows you quiz games, earthquakes, massacres, comedy shows, dancing elephants and state funerals all with the same level of seriousness. Television is like drink – you can end up under the influence. British television can range from the extremely good to the abysmal. American television is just abysmal. America is the only place in the world where absolute trivia is treated with such an air of seriousness, and serious subjects are treated so trivially.

American TV Show

Enter host (hair transplant, teeth capped, sagging face hitched back up by plastic surgery). Loud baying from invited studio audience reminiscent of Roman amphi-

172

theatre. Host waves charmingly. Howling and clapping continues. Time elapsed 47 seconds. After one and one half minutes of clapping, cheering and whistling host clenches hands over head in manner of man who has just run two minute mile. Women carried out, fainting.

Host   Hi there. (Shouts of 'Right on!' and 'Wow' from audience.) Welcome to the Eddie Braindamage Show! (Rebel yells and whistles from audience.) Are we having a good time tonight? (Shouts of 'Yes, oh yes' from audience.) So OK let's meet our first guest. He's been twice nominated for every media prize under the sun. He's a marvellous, wonderful, terrific person, and not just that, he's incredibly rich. Please welcome Mr Brooke Contradiction. (Screams, whistles, cheers, faintings, 'Oh wows' and 'Too muches' from audience. Enter Brooke Contradiction in white suede suit covered in rhinestones and salmon pink cowboy boots. He and Eddie embrace lovingly, shake hands, wipe eyes emotionally. Audience goes berserk.)

Host   Brooke, it's lovely to have you here.

Brooke   Well, it's wonderful to be here Eddie (whistles from audience) and I really mean that most sincerely.

Host   Well, that's really wonderful, Brooke. What do we think of that folks? (Cheers, from audience. Women visibly weeping.) Brooke, I'm gonna start with a hard one because I know a lot of people here tonight and a lot of people back home have read reports that said that your last film, *A Country Boy in 'Nam*, was too violent. Do you agree with this?

Brooke   Eddie, I'm American and proud to be American and I'll beat the living shit out of any one who knocks mah country, right! (Screams of 'Right on' and 'Burn the motherfuckers' from the audience.) When we made *A Country Boy in 'Nam* we wanted to show the real horror of that war. I played the part of a country boy from Tennessee who plays the guitar, loves his mom's apple pie, goes to drive-in movies and works hard on his father's farm. Then he gets drafted and blows the shit out of 12,000 Cong. It's a bloody story and sure we showed it like it is. Veracity-wise, we were as truthful as possible. For the sake of the film if a village had to burn, a village burnt; if children had to be napalmed, they got napalmed. We paid good compensation.

Host   How many people died during the shooting of *A Country Boy in 'Nam*?

Brooke   Roughly 36,000. We'd planned for less but there had to be a lot of retakes because of poor light, difficult lines and things like that.

Host   The press said the fact that you had a guitar with a built-in submachine gun and sang Johnny Cash songs while you gunned people down trivialized the whole attitude of the film towards war.

Brooke   The press are a bunch of hippie left-wing commie faggots. (Cheers, rebel yells and shouts of 'Burn the motherfuckers'.) We made that film because of all the dead boys that never came back from 'Nam. Good clean American boys who played softball and went fishing for catfish down the river after school. We made that film for them. (Sobs, howls, tears.)

Host   Well, Brooke, that's fantastic and stay right
there because now we're going to meet a dog
from Beverly Hills that has its own 12-
bedroomed house, 15 servants, a Rolls-Royce, a
swimming pool and silk cushions to crap on.
Here it is – Foo Foo la Mar . . . (Howls, cheers,
rebel yells, as yours truly runs towards bath-
room with hand across mouth.)

Television in Britain is not quite as bad as that. But
remember that it is run by businessmen on the commercial
side and ex-public schoolboys on the BBC side and we all
know how much they know about the real world – don't
we?

Sex on television

*It's too difficult. You might fall off and hurt yourself on the
floor* 'RED NOSECOMIX'

A lot of people complain about sex on television without
ever realizing how much violence there is on the box. Eye
gouging, biting, stabbings, blowing apart of people with
shotguns, rapes and murders – and that's just Worzel
Gummidge. If people are influenced too much by sex on
the television, the worst that they could do is go out and
end up in bed with someone. If somebody is influenced by
too much violence on television, the least he's going to do
is go out and hack someone to pieces at a football match.

Sex at football matches, by the way, is very difficult,
unless you're a goalie and all the action is at the other end.
You should then have enough time and something to lean
on.

TIME

Time past is contained in time future T. S. ELIOT
Piss off CONFEDERATION OF SWISS CUCKOO CLOCK MAKERS

All time is relative. The fourth dimension's own relativity
governs the dimensions of the other three: length, width
and depth – especially length which is why things often
seem longer in the morning than at night. Einstein also
proved that it was no use trying to measure things on a
moving train. This explains why money doesn't go as far
on British Rail as it does usually and also why their
sandwiches curl up at the ends.

TRAVEL

In this age of mass travel one place is getting to look very much the same as any other. The world has become a global hamlet with the same tight-jeaned, pimply adolescent serving the same Shamburger outside the Tower of London, the Kyoto Palace, the Pyramids and the Roxy, Cleckheaton. A stretch forward and a flick of the remote control console can bring the world glowing and second-hand into your living room.

Why bother to travel for the real thing? When you get there it's usually so full of other people who have got there that you can't get near what you got there for.

In the Forum at Pompeii on a package holiday once I watched stones that had stood up to the tremors of Vesuvius visibly tremble before the shock wave of a mass clicking of shutters belonging to a small invasion of Japanese tourists Nikonoclasm-bent. They all took identical photographs of the very same objects at the very same time.

Back in their front rooms in Kyushu, how many Sunday evenings will be spent in front of the neighbour's projector murmuring, 'Ah so! Déjà view!'?

Languages while travelling

An upper-class Englishman never learns a foreign language. He knows his own language is the best, why should he bother learning something inferior? The one phrase he needs to know in any language is, 'Do you speak English? Then fetch me someone who does'. LORD LONGDONGLE OF KLOOT

Lord Longdongle was beaten to death by an irate American waiter working in a Chinese restaurant in the Place

Pigalle. His attitude, however, persists, so that the world over bars echo to braying English voices calling out, 'I say, garçon, I mean charwallah, I mean boy, fetch me deux pintas de bierre. Chop chop, mein petite camarade, mucho pronto! What! OK?'

To which the reply usually is, 'Get stuffed', or some such.

Face facts. If you're English most of the world will hate you for what your grandparents did in the name of Queen Victoria and Disraeli, and before them every King and Queen we've had.

Countries England has been at war with

France
Germany
Russia
China
Holland
Spain
Portugal
Turkey
Italy
Iceland
Jenkins Ear
Tristan da Cunha
Christmas Island

Countries England has colonized and lost

America
India
Pakistan
Ceylon
Cyprus
Australia
New Zealand
Canada
Egypt
Rhodesia
Malta
Most of Africa
Borneo and Sarawak
Burma

Countries of doubtful allegiance

Ireland
Scotland and Wales
Yorkshire
Lancashire

As you can see from the above list, that leaves you about three countries you can go to without risking assassination or denigration – Hong Kong, Gibraltar and Krakatoa.

If you're American, you should be OK just about everywhere except Germany, Japan, Mexico, Vietnam, Cuba and Iran. Remember wherever you go they'll expect you to give them chewing gum, cigarettes and pictures of the Muppets.

UFOs

I've seem them lots of times, begorrah DELERIUS TREMENS, Roman Philosopher

So have I ARTHUR BEGORRAH, philosophizing roamer

If little green men land in your back yard

1 hide any little green women you've got in the house
2 phone the fire brigade
3 run

USELESS INFORMATION

Every true Armchair Anarchist should have at least three or four hundred bits of useless facts and information at his fingertips, they're useful for getting conversations started or stopped or just boring boring people. Imparted in the right way over a period of time, useless information can bring about the total mental breakdown and moral collapse of the strongest of personalities.

Examples of useless information

The shortest river in the world is the River Pnin in Yen Sing province, China, rising only 14 inches from the sea.

The most unusual coat of arms belong to Ron Slack of Barnsley who traces his descent from Slack the Tight, a wine taster and ale muller in the court of Edward II.

The fifty-ninth Mr Slack, at present employed by BR as a pie-hardener, has the family coat of arms displayed proudly above the front of his council house at Cudworth. It consists of crossed bottles with rampant ferrets on a green field. The bar sinister proclaims the family's illegitimate link with Big Julie, a stripper and courtesan from Manchester, who made the history books by earning Richard III the nickname 'Crookback'.

The world's most incredible escape story is that of Jean-Paul (Lucky) Robespierre who escaped from Devil's Island (the French Penal Colony) in 1938. He was imprisoned for life for stealing an elastic band in 1906. Unfortunately the elastic band was wrapped around 80,000,000 francs. After serving a few months he hit on a brilliant escape plan which took him 26 years to perfect. He decided he would construct a rocket ship and fire himself across the shark-infested waters to the mainland.

Over the years he stole spoons from the kitchens and made a rocket ship from them which he disguised as a palm tree. To power the rocket he needed gunpowder. He worked out that he needed a basic compound of nitre, charcoal and sulphur. The nitre he got from the nitrate salts in his own sweat which he dried out every day on palm leaves. The sulphur he extracted from the lice powder used to destroy bed pests and the carbon he got by working as a cook in the kitchens and burning everything to a charcoal. This resulted in so many beatings from his fellow prisoners that he went totally deaf, blind in one eye, developed a bad stammer, and a belief that the world was shaped like a giant mackerel.

Undeterred, he pressed on with his master plan. He had a fellow prisoner tattoo a civilian suit on his body complete with spats and a rolled umbrella and made himself a

British Passport in the name of Lord Peter Marchmont Giles, Third Baron of Winchelsea. He made a fuse from pyjama cords soaked in cooking oil which resulted in the entire population of Devil's Island sleeping with one hand holding their trousers up.

On the day he was to make his escape he lit the fuse, took off all his prison uniform and stepped inside the rocket. Instead of taking off for the mainland the spoon-shaped rocket merely circled the island setting fire to grass-roofed huts before landing in the prison compound and exploding.

The prison guards found a stunned and blackened English Lord inside the wreckage who, when asked his name, merely stammered. When the tropical rains fell and washed off the soot he was found to be wearing a beautifully tailored Savile Row tweed suit with slash pockets.

The French authorities returned him to England where he took his place in the House of Lords and a flat in Bloomsbury; and he once got drunk with Dylan Thomas in Soho for a whole year. His real identity was only discovered when he was knocked down by a brewer's dray and the police attempted to open his jacket to find his identity. He was sent back to Devil's Island where he died in 1957, still the best dressed prisoner they had ever had.

VON WANIKER, ERIC

Mystical researcher into the mysterious occult, Von Waniker found definite links between mould on bread, the London Transport symbol, Mayan rock carvings, jelly-babies and the costume worn by Buzz Aldred. He wrote such books as *Was God A Jelly-Baby?* and *The Omnibus of the Gods*. His study of Spaghetti Junction on the M6–M5 interchange led him to note its similarity to Celtic spirals such as those found on Irish passage graves and the plain markings of Narzac in Peru and prompted him to ask whether these markings were intended as messages for visitors from outer space. He found that viewed from above the motorway interconnections read GET STUFFED GREENEYED BUG MEN COMING OVER HERE TAKING OUR JOBS AND OUR WOMEN. A study of the shape of Blackpool Tower led him to the conclusion that its shape was that of a space ship and prompted him to write further books such as *Was Sandy MacPherson an Astronaut?* and *Did God Land on the North Pier?*

WOLVERHAMPTON___

The people of Wolverhampton, on the first Wednesday of every month, jump repeatedly into the air shouting 'Birdcage' – which seems to me a fairly good reason for not going there.

ZYLOPHONES*

The unfounded fear that strangers will ring you up.

The only way to stop your neighbour practising his zylophone is to introduce woodworm through the letter-box, or a woodpecker disguised as a letter holder. Either that or sneak in and spray it with rooting powder so that by the time he gets home from work, he'll have to hack his way through it.

*Ed   Er, as I said before, Mike, this is actually spelt Xylophones.
MH   It's funnier than zebras.
Ed   Aargh!